POWERFUL LISTENING
enhancing the impact of every conversation

Robert Lundin McNamara
1st Edition

Performance Integral

Performance Integral Edition

Published by Performance Integral, Boulder, Colorado.
www.PerformanceIntegral.com

FIRST EDITION

2 4 6 8 10 9 7 5 3 1

COVER DESIGN
ALEX MUSAT

LIBRARY OF CONGRESS CATALOGING-IN-PUBLICATION DATA

McNamara, Robert L.   1977 -
   Powerful Listening: Enhancing the impact of every conversation / Robert L. McNamara

ISBN-10: 0-9887689-8-4
ISBN-13: 978-0-9887689-8-7

   Includes Bibliographical References (Softcover)

   1. Adulthood—Psychological aspects. 2. Developmental Psychology. 3. Self.
   4. Cognitive Psychology. 5. I. Title.

Library of Congress Control Number: Pending

FOR LOVE

CONTENTS

INTRODUCTION

In this book we are going to explore the art and practice of powerful listening. Originally this was crafted with experienced coaches in mind as they develop more nuanced skills for enhancing the quality of service they can provide their clients. You may feel this bias throughout; however, in preparing this manuscript I've shaped this curriculum to also welcome a broader audience. You are encouraged to explore this book in creative ways that can serve your listening skills anywhere listening is happening. Any place better listening can help you mobilize what matters most to you and to the people around you are places I hope this book and its exercises can assist your most sincere efforts.

First, as I revisit this curriculum, we find ourselves facing significant challenges as a global civilization. COVID-19 has brought forth a global pandemic that has accelerated risk factors to life and civilization as we know it. Calls for greater ethical leadership and social reform have swept much of the globe as social unrest has sparked protests and demonstrations. A new era of diversity, equity, and inclusion may be upon us. However, national, political, social, economic, and racial divisions have been targeted and weaponized to create more challenging divisions amongst us. Civil discourse, the ability to simply talk to one another across differences, is in some key ways eroding. The shores of civilization are receding in some troubling ways.

As Planet Earth hurls through a vast unforgiving space around our Sun at some 67,000 miles per hour, we risk losing our abilities to cooperate with one another. While there's no evidence of life anywhere else in our cosmic neighborhood, it appears ever more challenging to recognize the precious opportunities we have as life on Planet Earth. And, as the only representatives of life that we know of in our solar system, our civilization lingers in peril because of our inabilities to cooperate.

If there is a time to invest in more capable listening skills in every sector of society, now might be a worthy time to do so. I fear if we do not extend more robust and generous listening to each other, across all of our differences, we may see conversations collapse. With the faltering of our ability to have real dialogue is the faltering of our first and only global civilization.

Second, to zoom into a much smaller context, listening is also a key management skill that leaders must up-level if they are to more effectively activate greater ethically aligned potential in the people and teams around them. If we are to coordinate efforts in non-rivalrous ways that usher in better futures for generations to come, we must all get better at listening to each other. Leaders must deploy listening skills just as parents and teachers are wise to mobilize this powerful vehicle for connection. Lovers and colleagues alike use the basic threads of how we connect, join, and cooperate. Regardless of the context and who's involved, we can all be served by better listening. And, we may be served to activate more powerful and capable forms of listening with some urgency.

This book introduces you to several key distinctions about listening as a whole. And our exploration together invokes some rigorous challenges, most notably that the way you listen may be reflective of an unexamined ideology that guides your behavior. To note, ideology, as we will be using the term, is a psychological process and construct, not a sociological one as Karl Marx and others have advanced. For us, ideology is a system of ideas and ideals that you author to create structure, meaning, and direction in your life. We can think of your ideology as an original internally directed framework, paradigm, or worldview. As we will explore, unseen ideological limits powerfully shape what you are able to listen to as well as how you listen. Lastly, these ideological limits can truncate what you and the people around you can achieve together.

As such, the curriculum we are set to explore peers into how you can more elegantly free yourself from the ideological structures limiting you. We will plant seeds and create opportunities for your listening to be and become more free. This means we look closely at how you can develop beyond your current ideological constraints.

Along our path we discover how you can develop powerful integrative listening skills. You learn how to use attention and awareness practices to support your post-ideological development. And together we will listen into less traversed domains of experience that may be enable you to activate greater possibilities within yourself and the people in your world.

At the conclusion of each chapter, you get specific practices to train yourself. It is critical that you do not merely read this book, appreciate the information and distinctions, and perhaps have some interesting insights. Activating these injunctions, listening in new ways, attending to different facets of your listening, and exercising neglected aspects of experience are more important than any idea, concept, or insight within the prose of this book. *The organizing intent of this book is to up-level what you do in your listening and to activate novel ways to work with your attention.* What you think about listening, what concepts, ideas and beliefs you have about listening are secondary. At the heart is a training to develop more powerful listening skills.

Here is a brief overview of how our journey unfolds through our book.

We have eight short chapters. Each one builds on its predecessors. If you leap ahead to Chapter 4 before reading Chapter 3, you will be missing key ingredients in our assembling of more complex listening skills. As such, you are encouraged to move through this learning sequence sequentially.

Here is a brief overview of your learning sequence:

Chapter 1: What Is Listening? Here we take an in-depth look at what listening really means.

Chapter 2: Listening & Development. We explore how adult development can impact listening and identify two core listening ideologies.

Chapter 3: Integrative Listening. We define and explore the foundations for growing what we call integrative listening.

Chapter 4: The Seat Of Not-Knowing & Curiosity. You gain insights into curiosity and not-knowing and install new ways of being that activate these qualities in your listening.

Chapter 5: Meditation & Selflessness. We explore the role of selflessness and how meditation can aid in the cultivation of more advanced listening skills.

Chapter 6: Ideological Activities for Growing Awareness. You get insights into the embedded ideological activities that are likely operating within you and many of the people around you. You clarify these developmental objects so that you can better listen for these dynamics.

Chapter 7: Listening & Simultaneity. You get visibility into the deep four territories of experience and how you can work with multifaceted domains of experience to evolve your listening skills.

Chapter 8: Obstacles in Your Ongoing Practice. This chapter closes our exploration by supporting your ongoing practices as we cover a handful of primary obstacles to your more elegant listening skills.

Again, putting your new learnings into practice, where it matters most to you and the people around you, is key. Research into adult learning and development has shown that it is essential that you exercise your new learnings, expand your choices, and change how you think, feel, and behave if you want to form new neural pathways and develop more complex and powerful capabilities.

So with that in mind, I encourage you to rigorously put into practice the new dimensions of listening that you'll be learning as you read this book. Attend to what my voice sounds like as you read this book. Hear each sentence as if you and I were in dialogue instead of skimming for concepts and theories. This way our time together through these pages can better be a more collaborative process where I speak and you listen. Then put into motion each chapter's practices and explore what happens, notice what changes, take time to feel into what's different. In this way our time together can be much more than merely an informational exchange.

When this developmental curriculum is coupled with your living practices and experiences, the result you will see over time is the emergence of a more mature and capable you.

With that said, let's begin!

Rob McNamara
Summer 2020
Desert of Southern Utah

AVALOKITESVARA*

By
Brooke Julia McNamara

This poem is listening.
In that sense it is open.
Each word

is the surface veil
of a tunnel of listening
with no end or origin.

It receives
the things we think we hide:
the shine of awkward posture

when performing power,
the fervid care - too vulnerable
to share - hiding under small talk.

It hears the sighs
of your fifty trillion cells
living lucidly under your selfing,

and it absorbs your gossip also.
Give it the headlines of the day,
and the ache to fix it all. Give it

the story of your little you
and all the elaborate plans.
The kingdom and the ash.

Give the secret crisis
that pierces the center of all
us creatures here on earth,

these tenderized hearts
wise to the verity
of incipience and loss.

Say your full formal name
and expect no echo.
Say yes

to yourself
and listen
to the listening listening.

* A buddhist term for someone who enacts the compassion of all
awakened beings and is often depicted as Kuan Yin and Kanzeon.

1.
WHAT IS LISTENING?

Let's begin with a simple question that has some not-so-simple answers: *What is Listening?* One answer is that listening is a process of perception. I create patterns of sound that you, the listener, receive and perceive as meaningful.

As you listen, you can hear the sounds each word enunciates. These waves of sound spark a constructive process in your mind.

As each word cascades through your mind, you are already embedded into images, interpretations, filters, and processes of organizing these sentences into meaningful information. Maybe you know me and have actually heard my voice many times before, so you can hear my tone and understand what I mean. Alternatively, maybe you've never heard my voice before. So I have a male voice with a particular resonance that taps into certain associations in you.

As you read this book, you can recognize that I am writing—or that we are imagining speaking—about concepts related to adult development, growing more complex skills, and expanding your ability to better understand, influence, and serve the people around you. And as you continue to read, the context of your expectations about this information, about me, about the impact on your work and life, will all continuously filter and organize what I am saying into information that is most meaningful to you.

All of this illustrates the two basic processes of perception. Perception is both the *organization of sensory inputs* and the process of *interpreting sensory information*. First, we have the processing of "raw" sensory input. Second, we have a joining and/or integration of sensory data with meaning-making.

So for the purpose of our inquiry, we can understand listening as an intricate meaning-making process and pattern of attention.

But the act of listening and being listened to has a great deal more meaning and value in our lives than this definition captures. Listening *connects* us. It is one of the most powerful faculties we can cultivate in our relationships with others.

Listening is also a door that enables you to *expand* who you are and broaden what you can take into yourself. When we listen well, we can transform relationships, cultures, communities, and even people's firmly held opinions.

In my experience there is no other faculty of perception that can connect you as intimately as your listening can to the people you live, play, and work with.

When I listen deeply, the basic boundaries between myself and others appear to change. When I am listening deeply to people, it feels as if I can plunge deep into the heart of who they are, as well as into where and how they are to become something more.

Professionally I am profoundly nourished by the robust intimacies and connections that I feel with my clients, colleagues, and mentors—to name only a few types of relationships. When done well, listening enables me to experience closeness and at times no boundary between us. And refreshingly, I find that how the people around me change is often connected to how I am changing as well as how we already collectively changing together. The people who I work with change me, shape me, and grow me in powerful ways as they develop, transform, and take new steps forward in their personal and professional development. Importantly, this virtuous cycle of transformation—which we will explore —is rooted in the type and quality of listening that is present.

Listening is also one of the ways we can grow and develop ourselves and the people we live, play and work with, as well as those in other areas of our lives.

Your ability to grasp who people are and where they are headed is essential if you are going to better mobilize change efforts. Whether these changes are to advance key projects, re-vision a marriage or company, create new ways to parent or change the ways communities come together you won't be impactful if you can't more robustly receive who people are and where they are headed.

Listening is what connects you to people's core perceptions, perspectives, and worldviews. It reveals the identities that people knowingly and unknowingly hold onto. Your listening enables you to sense into the seen and unseen intentions, agendas, and expectations that they are holding for themselves and others, including you. Through refined listening, you can perceive and recognize emotions, feeling states, and intuitions. And the quality of your listening is what can quickly reveal people's hidden assumptions, competing commitments, and central obstacles.

You and I are embarking upon a refinement of what I consider to be one of the most powerful faculties of perception. Your listening can have immense influence and impact in your social world. In order to navigate the socio-emotional landscapes within your many relationships as well as the socio-cultural landscapes of your life as a whole, first you must learn how to listen.

The quality and nature of your listening determines whether or not you are successful in your attempts to interact with someone. It influences whether your actions distance you from an idea or an emotion someone is experiencing. Developing your listening aptitudes is a practice that can unfold throughout your life. The cultivation and refinement of your listening has much to do with the ways you come to know the world around you, the people in it, as well as how you experience yourself. Through listening development you will find yourself able to enter into what people are saying more fully, and you will be able to draw out more valuable information from your communications.

Ultimately, our work together here is tailored to evolve these perceptual faculties within you. This book is designed to make you a more effective instrument of meaningful change and impact in our delicate world. And, refining your listening skills is also entangled in how fully you can thrive in your own path through life.

"LISTENING IS ALSO A DOOR THAT ENABLES YOU TO EXPAND WHO YOU ARE AND BROADEN WHAT YOU CAN TAKE INTO YOURSELF."

EXERCISE 1: REFLECTIVE LISTENING

The first exercise is *reflective listening*. Reflective listening is the foundation for all advanced listening skills. An elite athlete training every day will spend much of his attention on polishing the fundamentals. Similarly, you and I are beginning with one of the most important fundamentals in supporting others through listening.

Reflective listening is simple, which is why it is also a high art. But simple does not mean easy. Quite the contrary, it can take years of practice to elegantly employ simple yet powerful fundamentals.

Reflective listening mirrors back what has been communicated to you. This is not merely a reflection of what the other person said. Instead, your reflection illustrates what you received in his communications—including emotional and energetic tone. The better you can receive, the more valuable your reflection will be. And the closer you hug the contours of the person's meaning, the better you will be at reflecting back.

Here are 4 key steps for training your reflective listening skills:

1. Get still. Calm your mind. Receive with your whole body.

2. Listen carefully to what is being said. Attend to how people are communicating to you. Enter into the person's world. Join with his experience. Take in his ideas, feelings, and motives. Let go of yourself. Allow your awareness to soak inside of what and who is communicating to you.

Letting go of getting it right, suspending your interpretations, and not becoming overly invested in the exact words being used all can help you.

3. Wait.

Reflective listening gives room for the other person to share, express, and articulate. When you feel the impulse to fill space by speaking in moments of silence, take a deep breath and slow down. Instead of expressing more come back to stillness. Pause. Soften your belly, relax your eyes, and open your attention. Remember, your job is to receive.

4. Reflect.

Good reflective listening mirrors back the essential messages communicated. Done elegantly, it simplifies and clarifies what was communicated and what you both understand. In addition, powerful reflective listening itself communicates your interest, engagement, acceptance, and understanding. This welcomes a person into a more robust engagement with you.

As you start to train your reflective listening skills, revisit simple cues to anchor your intentions when you begin. For example:

- Just listen.
- What is being communicated?
- Note key words or phrases.
- Feel how people are expressing themselves.
- What's being expressed?
- Attend to the emotion and the energy in the words.

Simple, but not necessarily easy.

When you articulate what you have received, here are some helpful tips:

1. Avoid repeating what has been said to you in a rote fashion, especially if you repeat the message without matching your tone with the tone that was expressed. Nothing obstructs valuable connections faster than mismatched tone and energy. If you communicate to me with passion and enthusiasm or concern and distress, and I reflect

your messaging accurately but with a dispassionate neutrality, then I've lost you.

2. Use exact words and phrases sparingly. We are less concerned with a technical accuracy and more interested in expressing in ways that build mutually shared spaces of understanding. Using sincere reflections that make sense to you will be more trusted.

3. Be conservative with situating your reflections into your own familiar ways of perceiving and conceiving. Remember, this is your better attempts at entering into their world, not situating their experience into your world. When you take key communications and re-frame them in your own way of making meaning, it can muddy the clear reflections you are attempting to offer. This skill can take time to develop.

    For example, recently someone was talking to me about learning gaps amongst a team they are leading. They described efforts for addressing these challenges as succession development. Instead of reflecting back succession development, I spoke about the need to foster better institutional learning amongst the team. As it turned out, institutional learning meant something different for him and his organization. I quickly let go of my frame and returned to his language. Succession development was the pathway forward for our relationship, not the ways I thought about institutional learning. Sometimes your meaning making and reframes can help, but often they can impede better forms of listening.

4. Watch nonverbal cues. When your reflections veer off course, people will stop affirming what you are saying. Ask, "What am I not getting that's important to you?" Or, "How would you say it again?"

5. Ending your reflections with a simple question like "Did I miss anything?" can help your tremendously.

2.
LISTENING & DEVELOPMENT

In the last chapter, we touched on two facets of perception: the gathering of raw sensory data and the processing of transforming this data into meaningful perspectives. In our everyday experience, perception appears to more or less happen instantaneously—and as a result, we tend to assume that listening is a purely receptive faculty.

Notice how these processes are taking place right now. Likely there is at least some part of you that orients as a receiver of these words. My communications are leaping from this page and taking life in your own mind. Similarly as you listen to live communications of the people in your life, their words, tones, and expressions illuminate their experiences, perspectives, understandings, and identities inside of you. Listening is inherently a receptive activity.

However, we also know there is an active, constructive dimension to your listening. This means the meaning you are getting right now in this sentence does not purely belong to me. What you are experiencing right now is a result of our collaboration together—which is why we can also say that listening is a *collaborative endeavor*.

As you take in these words, with the sounds and textures you imagine in my voice, and the energetic resonance these words express inside of you, you are actively shaping and reshaping what I am communicating into your own understanding and experience. Therefore, what makes sense and what you value in this book thus far is part me and part you.

The same collaborative process unfolds when you and the people connect. As you listen to one another, the meaning that is established individually and shared between you is a constructive process of individual and shared meaning making.

Adult Development & Listening

I've devoted much of my life to the study of development. I've been delightfully captured in robust engagements with my own growth processes, helped others foster personal and professional development as well as supported institutional leaders fostering leadership and organizational development. My curiosity and commitment appear to endlessly fuel me. As such, when I embarked on designing curriculum that can help grow more complex and adaptive listening skills, I knew some exploration into adult development and how our own reference points shape our listening was important.

Exploring key developmental stages most adults operate in is important. First, development powerfully shapes what we can listen to in the first place. The constructive developmental processes that we're going to briefly survey determine what's heard and unheard. It can be eye-opening to realize that when we communicate across developmental levels—meaning, let's say, that if you are operating in a more complex stage of development than I am—and you communicate what is important to you, I may miss entirely what you most sincerely want to communicate to me even though I am closely listening to what you are saying. Second, development yields insights into why some communications clarify understanding, enhance connection, and build coherence. And developmental vantage points can help us unpack why other communications are confusing, erode connection, and build conflict in spite of our best intentions.

To begin, let's unpack how development can shape listening. As we will see, structures of development can illuminate useful insights into these inquires noted above. We will tour identity development as elucidated by Harvard University's former professor of Adult Learning and Professional Development, Robert Kegan. Kegan's developmental model, known as *Constructive Developmental Theory*, offers a powerful lens for investigating how development can impact listening. Three stages of Kegan's five stage model are relevant for us. We briefly survey the *Imperial Mind, Socialized Mind,* and *Self-Authoring Mind.*

Subject	Object
Elements of your knowing and organizing of experience that you are.	Elements of your knowing and organizing of experience that you have.
That which you are identified with, tied to, fused with, embedded in or otherwise possessed by is what you are *subject* to.	That which you can reflect on, look at, handle, manage, take control of, be responsible for or otherwise operate on are things that are object to you.
That which is subject is absolute and immediate.	That which is object is relative and mediated.

In the *Imperial Mind* stage, individuals are fused with—that is to say made up by—their needs, interests, and desires. If I am operating from the Imperial Mind, it is likely that my listening is going to be limited to my current needs, interests, and desires. You may speak to me about something important to you. However, what I am listening to is whether or not what is important to you helps me get what I want, what I desire, and/or what I am presently interested in. What's largely unheard is you, your care, and concern about what's important for you. In some ways I can't quite hear or receive what matters to you for you. As an "imperial listener," I can't hear what is important to you because the "sound" of my own needs are "too loud" or "too big." At this Imperial Mind stage, my need isn't really mine yet. My needs are not yet inside me. I'm made up by my needs and thus I'm not able to hear that you "have" something important to you.

Listening in this stage is in many ways embedded in these self-centered reference points. This means that as an "imperial listener," needs, interests, and desires determine what can and can't be attended to. When you are fully captured by a personal need, you can't see the need as an object. You can't manage or operate on the need. Instead, you are made up by the need. The actions this need puts into motion are who and what you are. You are embedded in the need. This is what it means to be "subject" to something from Kegan's perspective. So, if a need has you,

you will likely only hear what is relevant for you getting your need fulfilled.

While most adults aren't operating in the Imperial Mind stage, its essential functions are not left behind when we develop—they are included in later stages. This means the functions still exert influences within larger more complex identities. And, people's imperial tendencies do often show up under stress and duress. Research does provide evidence that your own imperialism can hijack larger complexities and collapse the scope of your listening into what only serves your needs, interests, and desires. And, developmental fallbacks, like returning to your self-centered orientations, are often only temporary and a necessary part of growth and development.

You might feel these dynamics at play when you consider the following questions: *What needs are most pressing and stressful in your work?* And, *what desires are motivating you in specific relationships that are important to you?* All of your needs, interests, and desires are influencing what you're able to listen to. The question is, how big are these influences? If we are operating from the Imperial Mind, these influences are bigger than us as we discussed above. However, as development unfolds, these needs, interests, and desires shift from subject to object. This is what marks development for Kegan and many other experts. When these core facets of our experience become objects that we can manage, operate on, and create different relationships to, we become less influenced by them. In short, we become less self-centered. This *decentration* as it is often called, or *recentration* as Kegan calls it, is a core process of development.

The next stage beyond the Imperial mind is called the *Socialized Mind*. Here, in this stage, individuals are powerfully controlled by their interpersonal relationships. In fact, if you are operating in this stage of development, you are made up by the interpersonal relationships that you identify with. Your sense of self—what you are subject to—is constructed from the interpersonal mutualities, reciprocities, and loyalties that you are immersed in.

No longer are you solely governed by your needs, interests, and desires. Instead you are governed by how your key relationships feel. You are compelled to take care of the people close to you by tending to their preferences and expectations, as well as their needs, interests, and desires. Why? Because to take care of them, to take care of these relationships, is to take care of you. In this stage of development, in some key ways, you are your close relationships. And thus we have key ingredients for the recipe as to why losing close relationships can be so ominous, devastating, and challenging. If you and I are really close, to lose me is also to lose yourself.

Similarly then, when we explore listening from this stage of development, your social loyalties—spoken and unspoken—erect boundaries around what should be listened to and what ought to be rejected. Your close interpersonal relationships, mutualities, and the reciprocities that tether the relationships that matter together powerfully shape what is welcomed and what is marginalized. Interpersonal relationships thus drive what's included, welcomed, and openly integrated. And, at the same time, cultural and interpersonal norms defend against differences that destabilize relationships.

Let's presume we work closely together and have many years of collaborating together. And, let's presume that we more or less agree that development is a good thing. It's something people should invest in throughout their lives. And, helping each other develop is often how we spend our valuable time together. Now imagine someone begins to share with you her divergent beliefs that adult development doesn't exist. She passionately assert development ends after adolescence. And, she expounds on the many reasons why investing in personal and professional growth is a waste of time, energy, and resources. She goes on to describe real change as a function of conditioning. And to put a cherry on top, she tosses out a few criticisms of your close collaborating partner Rob. Rob's behavior appears to be arrogant, out of touch, and aloof.

How might you feel if you are made up by our mutualities that are organized around development? How might you respond if the basis of why we connect and what we do when we are together is criticized as a waste of resources? Many individuals operating from the Socialized Mind would feel personally threatened in some way in such a situation. You may politely distance yourself from this critic to end the challenging interaction. Then you may discredit this critic when amongst close friends. Alternatively, you may embark on a fierce defense in the face of these criticisms. You may find yourself in a full-fledged conflict.

At this stage of development, we cannot yet listen to these critiques as merely differing ideas. Our critic may have articulated herself with respectful and careful uses of language. She may have been deliberate and intentional in the words she choose and the ways she phrased her critique. Yet individuals operating from the Socialized Mind in some key ways cannot hear the care and consideration expressed by our critic. If our critic took efforts to separate personhood and behavior, these differentiations may altogether go unheard. She may have been acting, from her perspective, out of respect to you and me. However, what was received, the impact of the communication, is likely to be quite different.

Living relationships, deep loyalties, mutualities that have us, regulate us, and structure us have been criticized. We likely feel as though our intimate and tender identities are under attack. Distancing and/or defending is thus often called upon. And while much of the critique was about ideas, some of the challenge was also about Rob. Yet in both cases, these critiques—these differences in opinion—are felt as personal attacks on a living identity. To insult, undermine, or critique what we do together, how we do it, and whom we are in relationship with is to challenge the very substance of how this stage of development experiences selfhood.

As you may be able to experience, when you are operating from this stage of development, you are in some key ways not simply listening as a separate and distinct you. You are not purely listening from your interests or desires. In a way your listening is formed by the cultures and the surrounding relationships you identify with and belong to. Your listening is inherently biased towards what we think, what we believe, and what we stand and advocate for.

For most adults, our socialized sensibilities—meaningful interpersonal relationships and the many layers of mutualities and loyalties— powerfully influence how they act and thus how they listen. A useful question for us asks again, *How powerful are these influences*? Is your listening largely made up by these social influences? Are you subject to these relational forces? Or, do you see these interpersonal influences as objects in your attention? Do you manage and navigate them intentionally?

What can be incredibly confusing for individuals operating from the Socialized Mind is when cultures diverge and we identify closely with both sets of relationships. For example, a new manager has been hired. You sincerely like your new boss; however, her way of operating is quite different. New expectations are being set. Different procedures are being put into motion. You trust and appreciate these changes when you review these together privately in a one-on-one meeting. However, in the team meeting, you're quite conflicted, uncertain, and unclear. Why? Because you know and can feel your close colleagues who are resisting these changes. Part of you moves with your new boss who you've quickly built good rapport with. Yet, part of you resists because of your colleagues. As a result you're quiet in the meeting. It is as if you have lost your voice. Internally you feel pulled in two directions. You are uncertain. How do you take care of two diverging relationships?

The *Self-Authoring Mind* often develops over time in response to these kinds of dilemmas and the limitations we experience as individuals operating from the Socialized Mind. In this next stage, individuals are identified with, immersed in, and made up by what Kegan calls self-authorship, identity, and ideology. Interpersonal relationships and mutualities become objects within the self providing new ways to be in relationship. Self-authorship brings forward new forms of authority, most notably an internal trustable authority. No longer is authority located outside of the self as individuals operating from the Socialized Mind stage orient. Instead of resting authority in trusted interpersonal relationships and social and cultural norms, a new inner voice provides discernments that are the trusted orientations for making choices.

The Self-Authoring Mind is, at the heart of its psychological structure, a self-directing and self-governing activity. This means that at this stage of development, you are made up by and immersed in an ongoing drive to shape yourself and your life to the images you form, your chosen values, your self-constructed purposes. This internally constructed system of governance is both the ideology that you create and the identity that you authorize for yourself and as yourself.

As you might imagine, this adds new layers to what we can listen to. This development reveals new dynamics that can be heard in communications that may not be explicitly articulated. For example, someone may reveal challenges she is having in a working relationship to you. She discloses missed deadlines, differing approaches to advance a key project, and an inability to get coherent around who's leading where and when. You may respond with something like "It sounds like you are trying to find your own voice here. Are you wanting to set boundaries on this relationship so that you can better mobilize your efforts more efficiently?" The person relaxes and says, "Yes, I wouldn't have put it that way but that's exactly what I feel like I am wanting."

Nowhere was this explicitly stated. However, listening from the Self-Authoring Mind illuminates implicit developmental dynamics embedded in transitioning from the Socialized Mind stage into the Self-Authoring Mind. As you might be seeing already, with each developmental step forward, we are better able to listen into developmental movements that aren't explicitly communicated. In other words, we can feel these developmental movements in the people we are in conversation with. By explicating them, by providing language to articulate unseen implicit dynamics, we can better help people through our conversations. We can support people's ongoing development by establishing shared objects in our discourse that illuminate emerging processes that can influence key challenges people are facing. In our above example, we can now talk directly about finding her own voice and setting needed boundaries on this relationship to better free up her efforts and effectiveness.

And, it's important to note, that when highly differentiated autonomy expresses refined boundaries with nuanced distinctions between personhood and behavior, identity and belief, and/or selfhood and personality structures, our less complex forms of development often cannot hear, listen to, nor understand these distinctions. As we discussed earlier, if I critique a behavior that you are subject to at any stage of development, you will experience this as a personal critique of you. No matter how nuanced my language may distinguish between personhood and behavior, you are fused with and identified as this behavior. However, if this behavior is an object that you possess, manage and otherwise operate on then you may more comfortably navigate my critique.

To give couple more examples, if I critique the ways that you always fall back on your own best sense making as the final authority to make decisions and you are subject to the Self-Authoring Mind, you'll take my critique personally. If I criticize the way a close colleague of yours operates and you happen share these same orientations you'll take this as a personal insult to you and your colleague if you're subject to this interpersonal relationship.

While self-authoring, ideologically driven forms of listening are much more open and flexible, they too are limited. The Self-Authoring Mind can be significantly more receptive to more of the human experience when contrasted against preceding stages of development. And, let's keep in mind that this stage too has its own defining limitations, biases and blind spots.

To illustrate how ideological reference points can color our listening, let us explore two common ideological constructs that often powerfully shape the quality and direction of our listening. As you will see, once someone has authored and refined one of these ideological positions, they will often be subject to each position's biases. My intent is to explore these as a means for empowering you to develop more complex forms of listening that can flexibly integrate both ideological dispositions. By doing so, you will be able to listen to so much more than if you were to be governed and defined by only one.

These two constructs surround all of us implicitly in our everyday communications. Share your parenting challenges with a friend or spouse and you'll encounter these constructs. Sometimes this listening ear will demonstrate one construct that brings you relief. Other times their listening bias may foster your dismay. Similarly, these constructs play out in conversations with colleagues, neighbors, bosses and the conversation you will be having with the auto mechanic. And, these constructs become far more explicit in the context of training and educational programs that develop interpersonal skills. If you've engaged coaching, counseling, or other management and leadership trainings that focus on developing skills for working with people, you have more directly encountered these constructs.

The first construct is what we will call *Narrative-Based Listening*—and it's probably the most familiar form of listening we do. Narrative-Based Listening happens when we listen with a focus on following the story or narrative of what someone is saying. The second ideological construct is *Feeling-Based Listening*. This form of listening is at work when we attend to the felt emotional and affective dimensions of communication. This kind of listening is less oriented to the narratives and more to the felt contours of how someone is expressing themselves.

Over the course of my own education and psychological training, I've encountered both of these ideological orientations. Narrative-Based Listening focuses on the use of language and the verbal behavior of the person speaking. The latter focuses on the feeling states and emotional contours of someone's experience. In my opinion, both are essential. Yet depending on who you talk to and the ideologies you've been immersed in, you've probably been exposed to the message that one of these orientations is superior to the other. Either listening for feelings and emotions are preferred, or thoughts and narration.

Remember, we want to make a developmental move beyond the binary constructs of either one, or the other. Therefore, I'll be supporting you to pursue a "post-ideological" relationship to Narrative-Based and Feeling-Based Listening. You can understand this as a possible developmental movement beyond the Self-Authoring Mind.

Two Forms of Listening

To begin, here is part of my story of how I was trained to listen within an ideology. In graduate school, Feeling-Based Listening was the mantra. This bias rippled throughout my graduate department with few exceptions. For instance, I can still vividly recall one of my counseling professors declaring, "All story is a defense against feeling."

As a result of my immersion in this ideology, the training I received privileged that the intervenor (the therapist in my context) would always direct the client's attention toward their affective states. I was educated that this was supporting our clients ability to "be with their emotions." This presumably was where healing occurred, according to many of my professors.

The message within this ideology was that what people said had less value than what was felt and experienced underneath their language constructs. Our clients' direct experience was considered more important than the interpretations and narratives that they might use to represent their experiences.

There are definite strengths to a Feeling-Based Listening approach. It can help stimulate the cortical density of the right frontal cortex, which is associated with the experiencing functions of the brain. And research indicates that these parts of your brain are associated with greater measures of joy and happiness. Furthermore, the ability to inhabit more direct modes of experience is an important facet of adult development—and Feeling-Based Listening is oriented toward this.

Steering people toward their direct embodied experiences—those that are not mediated through concept and interpretation—can be critical for many people's development. Additionally, gaining greater experiential flexibility—cultivating a robust ability to more nakedly experience the felt contours of life and then letting feelings and experiences go—can be powerfully useful in supporting people in advancing what matters most to them.

This kind of listening can further connects you with people's emotional states and underlying motivations. Attending here can improve emotional intelligences that often help people tremendously. Furthermore, your steady attention to feelings, affect, and emotions also helps vertically integrate nervous systems—both your own and the people you engage with. All of this can be powerfully helpful in both the personal and professional contexts that you and others operate in.

However, there is, of course, a downside to Feeling-Based Listening. Feeling states are almost always transitory phenomena. And because they are always changing, when we privilege feeling at the expense of thinking, we start to make narrative a dangerous road to go down. And when we presume, as one of my professors declared, that "All story is a defense against feeling," we set ourselves up to be overly consumed in the constantly shifting transitory feeling states of life. And, as we will see shortly, we miss out on other complementary opportunities to grow and foster more complex and integrated nervous systems which tend to yield more competent, caring, and capable people.

So on the one hand, while we might get better at feeling into the emotions of our lives, we also increase the risk of staying immersed in our feelings—without gaining perspective on them, understanding how they fit into the broader narratives of our lives. When this happens, this organization around feelings can become the operative dimension of our lives. The purpose of life and where we believe we are headed becomes more and more about having greater contact with our own experiential intensities. Put simply, this tendency runs the risk of fostering adult forms of narcissism and feeling based self-centrism.

Back to the story of my own education. After graduate school, I continued pursuing my passion for adult development. Over the years I encountered what I now appreciate to be some of the most complex and nuanced ideas about Narrative-Based Listening.

In contrast to what I was taught in my graduate studies, this other ideological orientation treated language as a reflection of how the mind makes meaning. Narrative and language, if studied closely and inspected with curiosity and nuance, can reveal developmental complexity. This is incredible if we stop and appreciate it!

What we place into our narratives, how we situate these objects in our stories, and also what we do not put into words can and does reveal the architecture of how we make meaning of ourselves and the world around us. This kind of developmental listening holds that what people say matters deeply if we are to know someone. We should pay attention to the stories people share with us. Listening ought to attend carefully to what words are chosen, which theories and models are used, as well as what perspectives remain absent.

Additionally there are other strengths that come along with Narrative-Based Listening approaches. First, it supports the brain's plasticity and ability to become more integrated over time. When we refine the conceptual nuance of our minds, it corresponds with greater cortical density in the left frontal cortex, which is considered by many to be the language part of the brain. As a result, one important form of neurological integration we can engage in is narrative integration. Gaps in people's narratives, parts of their life experiences not coherently held together by story and concept are quite literally gaps in their nervous systems. These gaps weaken people's nervous systems. Their resilience is compromised. The gaps also impact performance, overall well-being, and the level of human thriving people have access to.

When people have constructed powerful, meaning-rich narratives about their life, key events, and current activities, they are increasing their well-being and the level of thriving they have access to. This is all supported by increasing narrative integration. In short, narrative matters profoundly to all of us and in just about every situation.

And, there are, of course, limitations. One of the weakness of Narrative-Based Listening is that this form of listening predisposes us to remain trapped in language. Instead of experiencing the unmediated contours of life, everything tends to be symbolically mediated. And, for many adults, people are overly consumed by their narratives and abstractions.

Unfortunately, this means we risk missing out more diverse contours of human experience. Instead of direct experience, we often rehearse and repeat the same stories from the past. As a result, we remain encapsulated inside of our ideas, words, concepts, and ever-more-abstract representations of life and experience. Therefore it's no wonder research shows that individuals who are trapped in complex symbolic abstractions, and whose language areas of the brain are over-exercised at the expense of more diverse activation of and integration with other parts of the brain, these people report greater measures of depression and sadness and lower scores on happiness and well-being.

So to make sense of this ideological conundrum, I want to offer a few key suggestions. First, I really want you to note how the ideology of Feeling-Based Listening values emotion and the felt contours of human experience over the symbolic representations of the mind. This can often be an implicit ideal that is pursued in any given moment of how we attempt to help and support people. This ideological foundation shapes standards that we as friends, coaches, colleagues, and managers may be unknowingly conforming to. With few exceptions, we are likely shaping people to conform to these ideological dispositions if we fully buy into and invest in these ways of being and relating. Our biases towards prioritizing feelings and felt-experience are likely to influence the people around us.

Similarly, Narrative-Based Listening has its own set of values and complementary standards that may be guiding you and by extension the people in your world. Narrative, concept, language, and the construction of story are not to be interrupted. Rather, these should be clarified and pursued. When this ideal is operating, it places your attention intimately on the narratives people are weaving. The standards that are implicitly shaping your own experiences and relationships are ones that ask them to use words and ideas to ever better represent and explore their experiences.

Here are two points that we are wise to emphasize for your learning and development. First, the ideological orientation you bring to your listening powerfully shapes how you listen.

And second, how you listen—that is, where you listen from—impacts how you and the other people you interact with show up. How you listen and what you listen to powerfully influences where your relationships can and cannot go.

While each of the two orientations we touched on has strengths and weaknesses, we are wise to be able to appreciate both aspects of each approach. And, we are wise to refine our skills for leveraging each to help the people we are in conversation with.

Feeling-Based Listening can discourage people from creating new narratives with you. Narrative-Based Listening can discourage people from inhabiting and embodying affective and feeling states with you. Both might be helpful if someone is attempting to change. Both are likely useful if a community is grappling with something that's happened and how to move forward or an organization needs to innovate its culture and services to adapt to changes in the world and its workforce.

Listening is not simply a passive receptive behavior. How you listen, the shape and quality of your attention, as well as the kinds of things you are listening for dynamically and actively shape the social and relational space between you and the people you are in conversation with. Ideological orientations influence other people in your world. Unspoken and spoken social and relational loyalties impact the quality of listening you bring to the people around you. And, of course, your personal and professional needs, interests, and desires influence your listening and conversations. You, in just the presence and quality of your listening, impact how people show up with you and, as a result, what they will take out of your conversations and put into action.

In closing, this section on these two ideological frames on listening, I want to steer your attention back towards development. Behind each of the two ideological orientations around listening—the feeling-based and narrative-based orientations—there is often an implicit or explicit developmental claim. One claims that narrative and increasing complexity of language is more developed than simply attending to emotions and feeling states. The other claims that being able to perceive and attend to feeling without the compulsive need to narrate experience is a developmental move beyond the conceptual mind.

My contention is that neither claim is entirely true. Thinking is not developmentally more advanced than feeling. Feeling is not more developed than thinking. Both assertions are mistaken and reveal fallacies that distort listening, truncate relationship. and limit where we can go together in both our conversations as well as our other actions in the world.

Thinking and feeling, the cognitive and affective dimensions of development, are just that: two different facets of development.

Suggesting that cultivating our abilities for attending to emotion is more developed than cognition or that developing abstract thinking skills is more developed than working with feelings and emotions is misguided. *Integral Theory* proposes that these kinds of orientations commit a "level-lines fallacy." This fallacy happens when we place one distinct developmental line or skill domain on top of another—claiming that one is more developed. This creates a false hierarchy.

Thinking is not developmentally more complex than feeling any more than golfing skills are more developed than football skills. My quick example is obviously simplified to make a point—but the same type of impact arises when we make comparative assertions about the value of thinking versus feeling or vice versa.

Dimensions of development are distinct features that are often complementary to one another. Facilitating people's development requires that we differentiate different lines or domains of development from one another. If we fail to do this, we run the risk of erecting false hierarchies that rest upon not much more than our private preferences and biases. Skills and competencies that we prefer, are familiar with and value, are frequently judged to be more developed than ones we are less familiar with. Those who have a religious or spiritual disposition will often presume that faith development or the cultivation of first person direct verifications of realization are more developed than nuanced understanding of and ability to navigate organizational development. This is just as misguided as when a CEO with exemplary abilities to leverage interpersonal, cultural, political, and strategic perspectives to steer organizational outcomes presumes that her leadership abilities are more developed than any private spiritual experience may provide.

Ultimately, emotion frames cognition and cognition frames emotion in ways that likely exceed our abilities to understand them. Thinking and feeling modes of listening—and being—are both good, necessary, and useful in virtually all circumstances. Yet if we distort their values, and hierarchically arrange them in accordance to our preferences, we can do a great disservice to ourselves, the people who we are in conversation with, and to our collective opportunities for fostering greater flourishing.

So, let us not arrange thinking on top of feeling or vice versa. And, let's get curious about whether we might be doing this implicitly through our preference for an ideology of listening. In our next chapter, we'll explore a form of listening that makes a qualitative shift into a new level of development. But first, here are your exercises to support your next steps in evolving your listening skills.

"WITH EACH DEVELOPMENTAL STEP FORWARD WE ARE BETTER ABLE TO LISTEN INTO DEVELOPMENTAL MOVEMENTS THAT AREN'T EXPLICITLY COMMUNICATED."

EXERCISE 2:
INQUIRIES FOR GROWTH

As you have seen, development can powerfully shape your listening, which influences where conversations can and can't go. This steers your relationships in profound ways. For our next set of exercises, We'll be journaling, so please get out your pen and paper and find a quiet place to reflect.

If you're not able to journal where you are right now, I strongly encourage you to dialogue inwardly with the questions I'm about to ask. When you have the time and space, make a commitment to capture your key takeaways on paper. Reflection can be a powerful driver for many forms of development. Capturing new insights in writing, weaving them together with what you already know, and allowing novelties to find their way into how you are envisioning yourself moving forward all helps in fostering your ongoing neurological integration.

Take twenty to thirty minutes and reflect on the following five sets of questions. Pay particular attention to the questions that are enlivening for you. And, of course, invest in exploring related questions that have not been offered here but can be of valuable to you.

Inquiry Set #1
Which do you tend prefer—thinking or feeling?
What tends to get more emphasized, and why?
In what situations are you more biased towards feeling?
Where are you more organized around thinking?

Reflection & Journaling.

Next, let's consider some of your personal drivers that often influence—with varying degrees depending on changing contexts—how you listen, both to yourself and others.

Inquiry Set #2
What personal needs have been influencing where your attention is going?
How have your stronger desires been shaping you?
Where are your interests steering your energy and efforts?
How are these forces been influencing your listening recently?
Lastly, how have these internal forces operating inside of you impacted the people you have been communicating with? What's working? And what's hindering?

Reflection & Journaling.

Now let's investigate some of the preferences and tendencies that come from the interpersonal relationships, organizations, communities, and cultures you belong to and or participate in.

Inquiry Set #3
Who is most powerfully influencing the ways that you listen and what you listen for?
What trainings, courses, and certifications do you sense are presently influencing how you listen and what you listen for?
Who tends to activate listening for narratives, story, and concepts?
What relationships readily enliven you to feel more in your life?
Who best inspires listening for feeling and emotion?

What qualities of listening are the most impactful for you and the people you're in conversation with? What are the main reasons why this is working? What might be some of the blind spots or limitations?

Reflection & Journaling.

The next set of questions relate to your own tailored ideological preferences and dispositions. Consider the following questions to illuminate growing and/or well-established ideological dispositions.

Inquiry Set #4
Where do you listen for people's personally tailored philosophies on how to advance efforts and solve problems?
How do your ideas about the nature of change and its inherent processes influence your listening?
What standards, values, and ideals give you and your relationships direction?
Where do you most feel guided by your personal theories and the rules, boundaries, and regulations they provide?
What are the strengths and limitations of your ideological reference points? How do you see these impacting your listening?
How might a recent key conversation have changed if you had listened differently? What new listening skills might support you?

Reflection & Journaling.

Lastly, to finish up this section I am going to ask you some more additional questions that can support your development. Looking back on the reflections from the previous sets of reflection questions, reflect on the following inquiries:

Inquiry Set #5
Which influences tend to hold, direct, and more or less control the quality and direction of your listening?
Which influences feel new to reflect on? Explore how these relate to key areas that have your attention.
What situations may be important for you to leverage different forms and directions of listening?
What divergent forms of listening do you see yourself enacting?
What feedback is going to help you calibrate the kinds and direction of your listening?

Reflection & Journaling.

Next, we will expand on the flexibility and integrative scope of your listening as we open Chapter 3.

3.
INTEGRATIVE LISTENING

Subscribing to an ideology, regardless what that ideology may be, can limit the level of human thriving you have access to. While developing your own ideological dispositions can be life-changing and powerfully helpful, we are inherently a developmental species. You are designed to learn, grow, and develop regardless of what levels of complexity you avoid, demonstrate and aspire toward.

As such, freeing ourselves from our ideological limitations can be an important part of maturing ourselves and growing more valuable skills that can better support the people, communities, and contexts surrounding us. Freeing ourselves from our ideological orientations may yield more elegant skills. My guiding aims are twofold. First, my intent is to provide you with multiple ideological anchors such that you can more readily shape your own unique ideological stance in your listening. Second, I also hope to foster greater ideological flexibility. As we will explore further through this book, my high aspiration is to help you grow listening skills that are free from the limits of any one singular ideology— regardless of how integrative or inclusive an ideology may be.

What is most important for us here is the limitations inherent in your reference points—ideological or otherwise—are the limits of your listening. And where you are not able to listen is where you cannot go in the conversations you are having. To expand your listening is to expand the creative range and potentiality within all of your relationships. Evolving your listening skills such that you have greater range, flexibility, and more modes of how you listen and what you listen for enables you to foster more possibilities.

Now that we have explored two primary ideological orientations to listening—Narrative-Based and Feeling-Based Listening—we are going to shift into establishing a dialectic or conversation between these two reference points. By doing this, we may be able to construct a kind of listening that is not solely fixated in just one ideology. This is a form of what we will call post-ideological listening. The name for this form of listening is *Integrative Listening.*

Finding Yourself Between

What makes Integrative Listening post-ideological is that it does not exclusively subscribe to one ideology of listening. Kegan has conducted roughly four decades of research supporting the finding that we grow beyond the Self-Authoring Mind when we developmentally begin to operate on our ideological constructs.

Depending on where you are in your own development, you may still be in a process of forming your own ideological foundations of a more robust autonomy and self-guided integrity. Or perhaps you've already begun a process of differentiating yourself from your own self-tailored ideological orientations for how you manage yourself, engage in relationships, and manage your work efforts. Regardless of where you may be at in this particular moment, let's together imagine a plural you. A you that has many dimensions, faces, capabilities, and identities that resides between ideologies, people, needs, and so forth. Your starting point is an elemental betweenness.

Where are you? The many intelligences of the diversities of you take form and expression from your betweenness. And, to build on our conversation, your listening originates from a space between Feeling-Based Listening and Narrative-Based Listening.

Dr. Daniel Siegel, Clinical Professor of Psychiatry at the UCLA School of Medicine, talks about "balancing concepts and direct experience" in his exploration of how the brain becomes more integrated and mature. Like Kegan's, his work points toward a post-ideological shift beyond either Narrative-Based Listening or Feeling-Based Listening. Your more mature listening rests upon these more integrated functions of your brain and nervous system.

Where are you? *You're between.* You are in-between your robust abilities for language and your always intimate direct experiences. Somehow, you're both. Feeling doesn't pull you out of concept. Narrative doesn't unplug you from the felt-contours of your less mediated direct experience in the here and now of this sentence.

Because you're already between feeling and thinking, concept and direct experience, emotion and narrative, it's easier for you to train your fluidity. But the pathway to creating more flexible, free, and responsive listening skills is by exercising or training each with greater specificity.

Integrative Listening enables you to fluidly oscillate back and forth between these two modes of listening. First, attend rigorously to feelings, the felt sense of what is being communicated to you as well as the direct experiences of what people are living into as they speak with you. Then whole-heartedly engage narrative, concept, and theories. Engage new ideas that are being communicated. Pay particular attention to how people reframe challenges into opportunities, losses into gains, and limits into liberations all in the swift movements in language.

When you can readily vacillate back and forth between these two ideological dispositions without being unduly captured by either one, you've established a key process in the development of the more complex listening skill we're calling Integrative Listening. This signals a few key things. First, you're both recognizing and maintaining your betweenness. Second, you are embodying a more open dialogue or collaborative conversation between these two different kinds of listening. Instead of an ideological struggle or a collapsing of your listening into one or the other, you are becoming a more cooperative instrument for change. This larger creativity serves both you and your private interior life as well as the people you are in dialogue with. With Integrative Listening, you are able to harvest and move with more of the human experience in the moment. And, your listening is approaching a creative synthesis. Joining these two skills together becomes a powerful, dynamic, and attentive listening skill.

Now that you have a sense of the general developmental trajectory inside Integrative Listening, let's briefly explore how you can effectively build these listening "muscles." Just as you are between cognition and emotion, so too are you between every relationship, conversation, and situation that you are in. At times, the feeling dimension will take precedent while at others the narrative dimension will be more primary. As you toggle back and forth between these forms of listening and you become more grounded into these dimensions of your own experience, you are likely to find that the people you are in conversation with are more likely to follow you into these two different ways of relating, connecting, and taking action.

As your listening moves back and forth between these two different domains of experience, the people you are interacting with are more likely to create a greater balance between their own thinking and affective dimensions of themselves and the efforts they are advancing. This larger equilibrium that more readily includes and integrates more of the territories they are working with is a more generative place to relate, lead and manage from.

For those of you who are more practiced in Feeling-Based Listening, look for creative opportunities to challenge the people around you with more intentionally constructed new narratives, better ideas, and more robust theories that enable them to better navigate their obstacles and opportunities.

Listen for rigid or fixed narratives. Challenge these tension points with the aim of helping the other people to discover more nuanced and flexible ways of thinking. Where you see generalizations being made, push the person to be more nuanced with his language, encourage him to make more refined distinctions.

Similarly, if you are more comfortable and practiced tracking narratives and conceptual nuance, look for generative opportunities to start inquiring more directly into people's feeling states. This starts in how you listen for affect. Even as the people you're in conversation with supply concept, story, and discriminating ideas, steer your listening toward the underlying feelings, emotional tones, and felt experiences throughout.

Encourage them to make contact with the affective dimensions of their experience without prematurely placing language to it. Challenge them to make non-interpretive direct contact with their embodied sensations. Remember, your first intervention in supplying this challenge is for you to inhabit this kind of attention in your own listening with your own experience. It is less effective to cognitively direct someone to explore their felt experience while you remain analytical and discursive in your own mind.

Instead of filling your conversations with non-stop narration, invoke silence, reflection, and a greater attentiveness to present moment experience. Conversational moves could include something like "before we dive into the challenges you are facing, let's slow down and gather ourselves to find the strongest leverage points for advancing your efforts. Take a moment, what is the most difficult part of your experience right now?" or "I see you're moving fast, instead of describing what's happening, let's explore how everyone is feeling from your perspective. Let's start with you." This approach can help people more easily transition to affective, emotional, and felt experiences. Throughout, listen carefully to how you both respond.

Many of us in our aspirations aim to move toward the rapid oscillation between listening methodologies too quickly. Adopting this practice can give you the sense that you are developing more rapidly. I would like to encourage you to be suspicious of your desires for rapid developmental gains. These drives can be seductive and intoxicating for us who are aspirational in our drives to grow, develop, and yield greater impact.

When your ideas of where you want to be—or where you feel you should be—outpace your present day aptitudes, you run the risk of stunting your development, not accelerating your development. Instead of rushing to develop, I encourage you to focus carefully on your present day aptitudes and take small, creative risks that stretch you in meaningful ways. In this practice, simply focus on familiarizing yourself with the experiences and skills networked within Narrative-Based Listening and Feeling-Based Listening.

Growth can be awkward. Stepping into under-practiced and under-utilized skills often feels awkward. We feel as though we are not at our best. And it is true, you are not at your best. However, this is where you are more likely to learn and adapt. And this process of stepping into awkward under practiced facets of yourself is how your strengths, where you are most uniquely gifted, get networked into other areas. Over the long-term you become a more powerful instrument for service and change to the people around you.

One final point on enacting your courage to step into new areas where you lack polish, experience, and mastery. Welcoming and embodying your awkwardness, anxiety, uncertainty, and discomfort can be incredibly useful for the people around you. There is a good chance that people around you could also be served by enacting new conversations and actions they have less confidence in. The more willing you are to explore these difficult contours of your own experience, the less resistance and the more encouragement you will be able to provide others as they contemplate risking new actions that may be more valuable to all parties involved.

Returning to your own listening growth narrative (and take notice when you are transitioning out of the felt emotions of awkwardness, anxiety, and uncertainty), your expanding ability to fluidly and easily oscillate between Narrative-Based and Feeling-Based Listening fosters greater neurological architecture that supports simultaneity—that is, operating from both listening modes at the same time. This is what we discussed earlier as two distinct skills becoming one. No longer are you exercising one or the other. Integrative Listening fruitions as a singular creative synthesis of both forms of listening. Cognition frames emotion and emotion frames cognition, not as merely an organizing concept but a living experience of how you receive people in dialogue.

Take your time. Put in quality repetitions shifting back and forth between these two forms of listening. Don't unduly strive for this simultaneity.

Remember, adult development often doesn't unfold over the time frames our preferences often want development to follow. We are not talking about practicing for a week or a month. Most of us require tens of thousands of learning cycles to substantively grow the more complex neurological densities required. As such, the adaptive changes we seek are often slow, quiet revolutions in body, mind, and heart. Occasionally, development involves dramatic shifts. These come with their own challenges and pain points. However, the major dynamics driving development favor patience and persistence.

Integrative Listening 102

Those of you who have been intentionally exercising your listening skills for many years, if not decades, may already sense, feel, and recognize your abilities for executing Integrative Listening with nuance. Many managers spend over seventy percent of their work communicating. Coaches spend much of their time and energy listening closely. So much of life in general is embedded in conversation. If we look closely, we are immersed in generous opportunities to evolve our capacities to listen.

Our second task exercises abilities for attending to both ideological orientations simultaneously. So this task is designed for those of you who are further along in your skill development. Those of you who feel it's more appropriate to continue focusing on Narrative-Based and Feeling-Based Listening more sequentially can consider this part of the book as a roadmap of some of the territory along the road ahead of you.

While we have been using a developmental narrative to explore the joining of these two ideological forms of listening, I caution you in thinking about this skill as an abstracting idea. We are using narratives to open up growth pathways. However, Integrative Listening is not merely abstract sense-making operating on both domains of experience. Nor is this more complex skill a felt-sense that includes thought. These are developmental maturations and movements towards the simultaneity we are pointing towards; however, these miss the mark. They still fundamentally bias listening in one direction or another. Remember, the many facets of you live between. And, Integrative Listening truly flourishes when betweenness disappears. The implications of this are profound. As such, we are set to investigate these further in the chapters to follow.

Lastly, if you're interested in the research underpinning some of these developmental distinctions, I encourage you explore Bill Torbert's work in Action Inquiry Leadership. His substantial body of research illustrates how adult leadership development involves this move toward simultaneity. Additionally, if you're interested in the micro-developmental movements we are using to scaffold your listening growth paths, see Kurt W. Fischer's pioneering work in Dynamic Skill Theory, in particular his work in constructing skill hierarchies.

"WHERE ARE YOU? YOU'RE BETWEEN. YOU ARE IN-BETWEEN YOUR ROBUST ABILITIES FOR LANGUAGE AND YOUR ALWAYS INTIMATE DIRECT EXPERIENCES. SOMEHOW, YOU'RE BOTH. FEELING DOESN'T PULL YOU OUT OF CONCEPT. NARRATIVE DOESN'T UNPLUG YOU FROM THE FELT-CONTOURS OF YOUR LESS MEDIATED DIRECT EXPERIENCE IN THE HERE AND NOW."

EXERCISE 3:
FLUID TRANSITIONS

Your ability to shift back and forth between these two listening modalities rests upon your ability to make easeful and natural transitions. To shift how you listen and what you are listening to implicitly changes how you will respond. You will be off course if you are switching back and forth as a means of training your listening in ways that disconnect you from what matters to the people you are in conversation with.

Finding natural and easeful ways to navigate these transitions is key. Our intent is not solely to evolve your listening skills. The broader intention of cultivating more elegant listening skills is to expand your abilities to more fully welcome and mobilize more of yourself and the people you are in conversation with. Integrative Listening done well includes more of the people you are in dialogue with. As you are able to receive more, you can respond in more coherent, powerful, and meaningful ways that better support people in whatever they are talking about and whatever efforts they are advancing. As such, welcoming and accepting more of who is present and activating more coherent action stands at the heart of our intent to train listening.

If you can't make your own listening transitions naturally and with greater ease over time, you're likely to stop practicing regardless of my advocacy for you to explore new and awkward ways of engaging yourself and others. And, there are important social and cultural landscapes to effectively navigate. The people around you are going to be less likely to bring their more sincere concerns and aspirations to you if they keep having experiences of you being out of sync with them. As such, you need to be able to take risks to expand your listening skills and yet you must also maintain attuned. In short you need to be able to make fluid transitions. These are shifts in listening that will further connect you with the people around you. The transitions we want to avoid are the ones that create unwanted and/or unneeded disconnections.

To aid in your fluid transitions, we have two distinct practices. Each can be thought of as part of a bridge that connects Feeling-Based Listening and Narrative-Based Listening. Between these two ideological positions, we can practice *Narrating Feeling* and *Feeling Narrative*.

Both of these exercises can be practiced in flexible and spontaneous ways. However, I recommend beginning with more structured exercises. For example, commit to practicing one of these techniques for two minutes. Apply your undivided attention for the full duration of these two minutes. You could decide to employ one or both of these exercises for five or ten minutes. Regardless of the duration, keep your attention focused appropriately and stay engaged with the injunctions until you've completed your training cycle. I suggest starting with shorter intervals as opposed to longer ones. Additionally, I recommend that you do these two exercises back to back. For example, after completing a three minute interval in the Narrating Feeling exercise, devote another three minutes to Feeling Narrative. Training in this fashion will help you create fluid transitions within yourself. These neurological foundations will then provide greater fluidity of where and how your listening can be directed in conversation. Let's turn our attention to the instructions for each of these exercises.

Narrating Feeling

Narrating Feeling focuses your attention into the felt experiences in your body. And this exercise continually steers your narratives towards the immediate embodied sensations present. You are using language to specifically describe and label how you feel, what you sense, and where sensations are moving within you. Bring as much specificity and nuance to what you are experiencing in the here and now.

Here are ways to enhance the quality of Narrating Feeling:

1. Suspend efforts for creating narratives about what you're experiencing in your body.
2. Interrupt any pursuits to explore why you feel the way you do.
3. When explanations arise, turn your attention more acutely into the immediate sensate experiences in your body.
4. Steer your attention and use of language away from abstractions, hug the contours of the direct sensations.

There is ultimately nothing wrong with these explorations, inquires, and pursuits. In fact, you're encouraged to pursue these outside of your Narrating Feeling exercise. Narratives often fold back upon themselves. This means your stories feed more stories. When you ask yourself, "Why?" or "How?" narratives begin to explain origins and processes that are insights into what you're sensing and feeling. However, when your narratives fold back upon themselves, it is common for you to stop sensing and feeling into your current embodied sensations and this moment's felt senses. In short, your thinking can interrupt your feeling.

In Narrating Feeling, you are pursuing what is called a more vertically and horizontally integrated nervous system. First, we are connecting your prefrontal cortex's ability for language and direct experience. This is a form of horizontal integration in that the left prefrontal region is considered the language center of your brain. Your right prefrontal region is more responsible for direct non-interpretive experiencing. By joining these two together, we are fostering greater horizontal integration. Second, by directing both language and direct experience into the subtle nuances of moment-to-moment embodied experiences, we are steering attention down into the body. When attention can include, investigate, and rest in your somatic experiences, we are fostering the vertical integration of your brain and nervous system. As such, to maximize your benefits from this exercise, keep joining present moment experiences with the deliberate use of language to narrate the most elemental felt senses in your body.

Feeling Narrative

Feeling Narrative focuses your attention into the felt experiences of your mind's activities. This exercise, as you might already sense, steers attention into your narratives; however, you are including or welcoming your whole body and felt experiences into your thinking. Here you use feeling and felt senses to bring more energy and nuance into your ideas, beliefs, concepts, theories, and stories. Bring as much feeling as you can into the narratives you are animating in the present moment.

Here are ways to enhance the quality of Feeling Narrative:

1. Enter more fully into the free movements of your narratives.
2. Pay close attention to how specific words and phrases feel.
3. Allow your body to feel the assertions, changes and questions that arise in your narratives.
4. If feelings suspend your narratives, return back your narratives. Ask yourself simple questions like, What's happening? Who's involved? Where are things going? What are my opinions? What agendas are present?

Once again, there is nothing wrong with the free movements of your feeling-based experiences that are non-interpretive. And, as noted in Narrating Feeling, pursue these experiences outside of this exercise. As you might already be seeing, we are pursuing the same vertical and horizontal integrations; however, we do so by emphasizing different dimensions. Just as thinking can interrupt feeling, feeling can interrupt thinking. To weave a more integrated mosaic between these often disconnected worlds is to work towards a greater felt embodiment of your narratives, concepts, theories, ideas, and stories.

Together these two distinct practices, Narrating Feeling and Feeling Narrative, empower you to foster more easeful transitions between Narrative-Based Listening and Feeling-Based Listening. As we discussed, over time these two skillsets can become one simultaneity. You become a more elegant and coherent listener through Integrative Listening. However, the evolution of your listening also likely integrates other key skills. This has certainly been my experience. It is to some of these additional skills and training methods we now turn our attention.

4.

THE SEAT OF NOT-KNOWING & CURIOSITY

Sigmund Freud, one of the greats of Western psychology, presents us with a paradox. He is both widely studied and, in many circles, largely discredited. Yet in the realm of coaching, psychotherapy, psychiatry, and other types of interpersonal mentorship, his work continues to offer critical insights about the therapeutic and transformative processes we are engaged in.

One of Freud's great contributions can be found by looking into how he prepared himself to listen to his clients. His inner preparation is an essential learning in our exploration of the refinement of listening. Even if your ideology inclines you to be skeptical of Freudian approaches, I encourage you to openly explore the insights Freud has to offer us about how we can better listen to the people around us.

Freud understood listening to be a form of joining. And in order to join with his clients, Freud believed that he needed to establish what he called the suspension of the critical faculty. We can think about the critical faculty as an ongoing conceptual analysis. It's our assessing, critiquing, and interpretations on what and who you are listening to.

As you may already be sensing, we are not simply talking about Narrative-Based Listening here. Freud is talking about an addition. Something extra that may not be necessary to be added. The critical faculty is something more that can, at least at times, get in the way and interrupt more robust forms of joining.

This addition would mean that you're not in a more elementary way just listening. You are also judging, discerning, critiquing, and otherwise commenting on what you've just received. For people earlier in their listening development, as soon as the internal commentaries begin, they can stop listening. More energy may quickly become invested in making sense of what's been shared, instead of remaining more open and available. The critical faculty might begin attending to the ways they want to respond.

Whether you're a coach, manager, parent, or good friend lending an open ear and a curious mind as you attend to people's concerns, there is often a felt pressure to respond well. In many contexts, we are biased towards knowing. We often like to be certain, clear, and insightful. This can be readily felt when someone brings sincere challenges, questions, and concerns to us. When you are implicitly or explicitly asked to provide advice and direction, many of us feel pressures to respond well. This demand to answer well with clarity and insight that is of great value can swiftly interrupt or collapse listening.

When we've had many years of listening practice, we often gain the ability to listen to both to the commentaries, interpretations, and analysis within ourselves while also maintaining an open receptivity to the people we are in conversation with. We'll return to this later on as this is a developmental skill we will mature together. However, the foundations of elegant listening require us to listen beyond our ideological constructs and the interpretations that follow. We need to be able to at least suspend and sustain a more radical openness if we are to activate the more powerful gifts of listening.

Suspending the critical faculty enables you to nurture a much more powerful and impactful openness. When you suspend your own narratives, concepts, models, and the ideological dispositions that tend to dictate your thinking and action, your attention can stay more open. You can choose to be more available. You can more readily join. And, it is within this broader attention and more free awareness that you can better leverage both Narrative-Based Listening and Feeling-Based Listening.

In Freud's view, the conceptual analysis that happened while he was with his clients was understood as a form of defense against making more full forms of contact with his clients. To remain internally active while we are listening risks losing more potentiated forms of joining the people we are with.

Many coaches today are trained in one or more coaching frameworks. Each supplies implicitly and explicitly methodologies directing what you are supposed to do. This, of course, shapes the kinds and directions for your listening. This helps coaches situate their clients' processes, lays out next steps, and helps structure the relationship. These can all be helpful in a broad range of situations. The same can be said for how leaders and managers are trained formally and informally. Even couples operate in frameworks they've been trained in to help navigate challenges. But these ideological structures often limit both a recognition of and creative responses to novelty. It is as if our minds have already been biased towards fitting everything into preferred or familiar models and frameworks. We risk prematurely situating our conversations into prefabricated molds, molds that miss creative, unique expressions. Our learning and direction in contrast leans us towards listening from a more open and uncertain presence.

Navigating the Trap of Knowing

While training is obviously essential, a sizable portion of the conceptual and analytic activities we engage in while we are presumably listening are likely interruptions—and perhaps defenses—against more powerful ways of joining. These movements inside of you are often mistakes. Of course, the critical faculty can also yield incredibly valuable learnings. The polished and practiced transfer of knowledge is not to be denied or undervalued. As noted earlier, we'll return to these possibilities later. For now we follow Freud's instruction as a means of building different skills that will, in the end of our curriculum, join together as more elegant expressions of how you listen and join.

Let's continue our pursuit to listen in more radically open ways that are not subsumed by our training, expertise, or experience. Let's invest in listening spaces that are beyond your known and practiced ideological formations. In order to cultivate this more radical space within yourself and to be discovered by this openness between you and those who you are listening to, you must navigate what I call the *trap of knowing*.

The trap of knowing is simple but not easy. When you assume to know someone, you've been caught. When you assume to have received completely what was communicated to you, you are caught. When you arrive at certainty, you have been captured by the trap of knowing. In short, when knowing has you, you've been trapped.

Now I sincerely hope you listen deeply to come to know someone with profound clarity. I want you to give people potent experiences in which you do intimately get them to a place where they feel held, received, trusted, and cared for. And, I hope you are able to co-construct great clarity, certainty, and knowledge with the people around you. A lot depends on us doing this together.

However, my challenge here is that no matter what, regardless of where you arrive, your listening remains open. Do not allow your uncertainty and curiosity to collapse. In the face of personal certainty, remain open to further possibilities. As you experience robust knowledge and wisdom, foster not-knowing. In the face of the utterly familiar and ordinary, brighten curiosity.

Not-knowing is a form of fundamental curiosity. It is a leaning into new and different kinds of experiences. Curiosity has been shown to be a significant driver of potential in organizational settings. And, curiosity drives meaningful engagement within your personal relationships. When you are curious, you actively seek out and more readily engage with new and divergent forms of knowing and relating. When you have established robust forms of curiosity, you more sincerely engage honest feedback, especially when it does not fit how you know and understand yourself. Your curiosity is already joined with and engaged as an open uncertainty, an intimacy with what is happening in the here and now, and curiosity better integrates diverse forms of novelty.

Importantly, not-knowing is not opposed to any facet of what, who, and how you know. All these are welcomed, often eagerly. Instead of satisfaction, satiation, and/or intoxication with knowing, not-knowing as you is simply committed to seeking more. Unattached and freed from the contentments, satisfactions, and completeness that fill a less curious mind and heart is a more potentiated incompleteness, a radical unbounded hunger that continues to sense into the edges of what's not known, unclear, or possible. Listening from not-knowing implicitly leans into the conversation quietly asking, *What else? What's more? What's different? What's hiding? What's almost here?*

Not-knowing is not simply a mental exercise. Rather this is an openness and curiosity living in your body, mind, and heart. In contrast to people who are consumed by their knowledge—that is they are subject to it—

and are thus predisposed to defend it and themselves, when you are subject to not-knowing and curiosity there is often an innate joy and passion for learning and exploration. As a result, ever deeper, more information-rich, and experientially diverse connections come about to be creatively and joyfully explored in dialogue. But these pleasures are granted for those who first dare to take risks and explore out past the boundaries of the familiar and comfortable.

When you listen from these greater forms of curiosity that move with and from more of you, you're able to "hear" more and as it turns out this enables you to move more. You can sense more of what is going on within the people you are listening to. You can better feel where people's innate motivations are going, how they might enact new pathways to advance valuable efforts, and what emergent possibilities are ripe.

To the degree from which you can embody this fundamental curiosity, not-knowing, and spaciousness, you are expanding the location from which you can listen from. We can imagine this as a vast seat from which you can listen, one that is more liberated from your more familiar ideological dispositions. And, building on Chapter 3, your sincere curiosities can be effective ways to fluidly navigate thought and emotion.

Don't Get Limited by Conceptual Certainty

While clarity and certainty can support you in many situations, these can work against your better efforts. It can be helpful to note that in cultivating not-knowing, brightening curiosity, and expanding the open space from which you can listen from, these too can become fixations. As such, in growing these skills, it is important for you to be nimble. You are encouraged not to cognitively commit to a sense of knowing or possessing uncertainty. We are less interested in grasping hold of these qualities as concepts.

Gaining conceptual clarity on not-knowing misses the more essential point of you becoming *more curious*. Looking at not-knowing, curiosity, and spaciousness is different than being and embodying these qualities. While creating a clear understanding—a third-person objective perspective—can help at times, these vantage points that "operate on" not-knowing and curiosity are not the first-person immersion into these qualities as you. To briefly note, an intentional immersion into or confidence in being made up by not-knowing and curiosity is an altogether different vector of development than what we explored in Chapter 2. As you may recall, identity development involves shifting that which we are subject to into an object to be managed. Here we are intentionally going in what can be understood to be the opposite direction. Your more complex listening skills welcomes the abilities for being subject to the qualities of curiosity and not-knowing.

As such, if your mind is saying to you, "Okay, not-knowing and curiosity, I've got these now," be suspicious. These kinds of movements could very well be some of the basic activities Freud might have considered to be your critical faculty. And, these objective reference points very well may interrupt more powerful forms of joining with the people you're listening to. So, gain greater clarity. Certainty will be essential at points in your conversations. However, I encourage you not to get overly seduced by your mind's capability to hold, think, and otherwise operate on these qualities as purely abstract concepts. Remember, you are after an intimate enactment as an embodiment of these qualities. Don't limit yourself and your listening by staying in an abstract orientation towards listening. Your more elegant skills likely require you to be and become made up by a greater spaciousness, not-knowing, and curiosity.

"THE TRAP OF KNOWING IS SIMPLE BUT NOT EASY. WHEN YOU ASSUME TO KNOW SOMEONE, YOU'VE BEEN CAUGHT. WHEN YOU ASSUME TO HAVE RECEIVED COMPLETELY WHAT WAS COMMUNICATED TO YOU, YOU ARE CAUGHT. WHEN YOU ARRIVE AT CERTAINTY, YOU HAVE BEEN CAPTURED BY THE TRAP OF KNOWING. IN SHORT, WHEN KNOWING HAS YOU, YOU'VE BEEN TRAPPED."

EXERCISE 4:
PHENOMENOLOGICAL REFLECTION

Phenomenological Reflection is a powerful writing injunction that can evolve your reflection and writing skills. As you will see, this injunction helps you listen in more open and curious ways to yourself. When employed regularly, this tool develops powerful skills employing more rich forms of Integrative Listening with the people you are in conversation with.

Phenomenological Reflection can be thought of as a bridge between your more typical narrative-based reflections and a meditative state of awareness. We will explore meditation in Chapter 5 in greater depth, but for now we can focus on a mindful meditative state. Mindfulness is a unique synthesis of curiosity, openness, and acceptance all colored by a warmth or kindness towards all facets of your experience. If narrative-based reflections involve a full immersion into your stories, narratives, distinctions, and so forth, mindfulness is a broad open awareness that warmly witnesses all of our moment-to-moment experiences without actively engaging any phenomena. Phenomenological Reflection is a fluid shifting back and forth between these two different ways of functioning. You are doing this properly when you can maintain this middle range. You don't fully immerse into the narratives. Nor do you fully immerse into a mindful state. Remember, you're in-between.

Phenomenological Reflection is best employed first as a writing modality. I first learned of this as a journaling exercise. You'll employ this tool first in your written reflections. However, as you grow skills to enact this synthesis of mindful awareness and narrative-based engagement, you'll likely notice this way of functioning being employed in other areas of your life. And, of course, my hope is that the neurological foundations that enable Phenomenological Reflections to flourish will bolster the quality of the Integrative Listening you can animate with people when in dialogue.

Step 1: Select a valuable area of your life to reflect on.

You can employ Phenomenological Reflection on any facet of experience. However, I encourage you to train theses skills focusing on what matters most to you. Consider what has ultimate significance for you? What are the most valuable facets of your life that you can make contact with? Trust whatever surfaces in your greatest sincerities and move forward with this.

Step 2: Begin Journaling.

Whether you open up a document on your computer, or grab a piece of paper or your journal and put pen to paper, begin to capture your thoughts.

Sense into this area of significance. What is it that you want to say? What is already being said inside of you? Begin to articulate and express this narrative or these narratives. Capture these thoughts. Articulate your questions, insights, and/or findings. Draw, diagram, and/or narrate. Regardless of the forms your reflections take, create an artifact that reflects what matters to you right here and now.

Step 3: Pause, Sense, and Feel.

Stop writing. Open your awareness and listen inwardly. Sense into your felt-experiences. Attune to your aliveness. Feel into what is most vital in this precise moment.

In the suspension of your writing, you are differentiating attention from the narratives you have just laid down. And, you're separating your engagement from articulating your next idea, thought, or word. Instead you're steering your engagement towards your open attention and broadening curiosity. You are transitioning from thinking towards feeling and sensing. You aren't leaving your narratives, but you are tuning into your more raw experiences.

There is an intent though. You are sensing for the living threads of narrative that can potentially unfold what matters most to you. You are searching for the naked felt senses of aliveness. And you yearn to yoke this into language.

Step 4: Write.

Infused with your less-mediated direct experiences of what is moving you, begin writing again. Freely express and articulate. Diversify. Take risks. Say something new. Express it again differently. Open up new pathways. Be creative.

Sometimes returning to your writing will have great coherence to where you paused in your narrative. It is as if you suspended writing and rooted into your more direct and immediate felt experiences of aliveness and are conducting this vitality back into a coherent narrative. Other times you will return to writing into an entirely different narrative. We are not journaling to create coherent narratives that flow seamlessly from start to finish. Instead we seek to create and weave narrative from the more elementally felt experiences of your creative aliveness.

Step 5: Flicker Back and Forth.

There is no set prescription for how long to do Step 1 and Step 2 before you do Step 3. You could journal for a few minutes and then pause. Or you may write for ten minutes before you pause, sense, and feel into more your direct experiences. Similarly you could spend forty seconds or eight minutes in Step 3. Trust your own timing.

And, steer your Phenomenological Reflections towards shorter periods of vacillating back and forth between sensing inwardly and expressing. Over time you'll begin to see narratives organically commingling inside of your pauses, and you'll sense and feel into your larger vitality while you're in midstream expressing a sentence. These are markers that your Phenomenological Reflections are maturing.

And, hopefully you see some of the overlapping similarities with the skills we've been developing. Phenomenological Reflection will enhance your ability for Narrating Feeling and Feeling Narrative. Yet there are two ways that Phenomenological Reflection differs from the exercises in Chapter 3. First, you don't need to be symmetrical with how long you spend in Steps 1, 2, and 4 with how long you are in Step 3. Again trust the flow and timing that feels right for you. Second, Phenomenological Reflection is invested in creating reflective artifacts. Narrating Feeling and Feeling Narrative are exercises that do not create artifacts. Chapter Three's exercises are purely interior injunctions.

Together, we're providing diverse contexts for similar learning cycles to occur. When regularly employed over time, you will be grooming more complex connections within your brain and nervous system. These foundations will begin to take shape in your social perceptions. These injections within yourself are evolving your ability to perceive more acutely into all of your interpersonal relationships. And, as you'll begin to see as you put these exercises into regular motion, they will advance the skill of your listening.

5.
MEDITATION & SELFLESSNESS

In the last chapter we looked at how the critical faculty of our analytic and objectifying mind can impair listening and erode key abilities for joining with others. We invested in practices and potentialities for cultivating a more radical openness that is fueled by your sincere curiosities. By suspending your mind's more automated judgements— that is to say, by sidelining your discernments that locate conversations squarely into the known contours of what you already know—there are greater possibilities for you to listen more fully with more of yourself.

To build on the foundations of not-knowing and curiosity, we turn our attention now towards meditation and some key discourse around being and becoming more selfless. Your more complex and elegant listening skills may very well depend upon these powerful practices and actualizations. To begin, two underlying drivers bring us into the practice of meditation.

First, meditation can be a powerful tool for advancing adult development. And, as we explore here, the more learning cycles you have in dropping your own self-referential patterns, the better you will be able to listen. Enduring and reliable listening skills capable of penetrating into the heart of people and situations with curiosity and nuance is dependent upon your ability to drop yourself as a focal point.

Second, meditation can be a powerful vehicle for stabilizing your access to a more fundamental openness. As we are set to explore, this openness is not dependent upon the contents or activity of your mind in any given moment. Meditative training can yield a vast availability and radical openness that is undisturbed by any of the typical movements that command our attention, energy, and engagement. Meditation, when practiced properly, can help you warmly welcome and skillfully navigate more meaningful and valuable possibilities.

Developmental Catalysts for Constructing Skills

Let me begin by emphasizing that meditation *can be* a developmental catalyst for certain forms of complexity. Meditation does not appear to be a universal driver of adult development. Connect with an advanced meditation practitioner who's spent a quarter of a century diligently sitting in a monastic setting that does not exercise social skills, and you are likely to feel these interpersonal gaps. My observation here is that meditation can hold you back just as much as any other activity that may over-exercise and reinforce already established skills, traits, and ways of being. This potentiated activity brings with it risks for interrupting other forms of learning and development that may also be important. And, with that said, many forms of meditation can foster key developmental shifts that can profoundly help us as we navigate life, death, purpose, and relationship. For our purposes of growing more advanced listening skills, the practice of meditation can be an important tool.

The first skill that we are interested in developing is the stabilization of attention. What this means is that you are able to place attention into the here-and-now and keep attention resting here. The better your attention can abide in the present moment, the more stable and concentrated your attention is. The second skill is the openness of your attention. Developing openness through your meditation training means that the posture of your attention becomes progressively more receptive and spacious. These are two meditative skills that can be developed over time.

Stabilizing attention is often achieved through concentrative meditative training. Let's say you meditate for twenty minutes and you can unwaveringly count your breaths from one to ten in an unbroken succession for the full duration of the meditation. At this level, we could say you've developed an intermediate level for stabilizing attention. As such, you can keep attention in the here-and-now as it pertains to your breath quite well. If you cannot count your breaths from one to ten without your mind wandering off for a meaningful duration then, more concentrative meditation training may be helpful.

Now, counting your breaths isn't necessarily going to help you listen to someone else with greater nuance. Cultivating greater attentional stability may very well help—it often does—but this private meditative skill might not translate into better social skills. One of the developmental challenges we all face is learning transfer gaps. When we first learn a skill, we learn it in one context. Being able to demonstrate this skill in different contexts is a more complex task when compared to repeating the skill in the same learning environment. Thus, in our developmental journeys, we initially are not able to transfer new skills into different contexts. So you may be able to effectively stabilize attention into the present moment as you meditate; however, you may not be able to stabilize attention into the here-and-now as you socially engage in conversations.

This is also true for developing an open and receptive posture of attention. Can you meditate for twenty minutes while keeping attention broad, open, and receptive? Can you train yourself such that no matter what arises in your experience, your attention does not collapse on or into some narrowed part or feature of experience?

Duration can be used as one measure of maturity here as we noted above in discussing stabilizing attention. However, we could also assess skill complexity in terms of the scope or scale of openness. Development may begin with an open mindful attending to the contents and activity of the mind. By exercising *mindsight*—the sense perception of how you experience your own mind—you gain greater openness to the movements of your mind without becoming subject to or engaged as the activities of your mind. A more open posture would be to integrate mindsight with *interoception*, the somatic sensing of the body's sensate experiences. If you can welcome both domains of experience at the same time, we can say you've developed a greater openness. And we might continue building openness outward, meaning we join what's happening in body and mind with what's unfolding in the surrounding environment. Or we may expand openness inwardly where we begin to include silence, stillness, or formlessness. To include these may be considered to be more developed than an openness limited to just body and mind.

With thousands of learning cycles—that is to say, practicing meditation in an ongoing way—these skills will become ever more networked together. First stabilizing attention, then opening attention. Opening attention, then stabilizing attention. Back and forth you enact these skills in your meditative training. Over time these become one coherent skill. And, once you are able to transfer this skill into entirely different environments and demands that, at least on the surface, have nothing to do with meditation, you've developed more powerful skills. You have become more developmentally complex.

This is one way we can construct meditations that are tailored to our learning and development. By architecting practices that grow skills and networking these skills together, meditation can be powerfully catalytic.

And, I hope you can also see some risks here. If you train and develop in one area, you aren't in others. Even expertly crafted meditation injunctions have weaknesses and blind spots. Thus, we need some cross-training sensibilities as we think about meditation and its ability to foster development. In short, you are wise to train integrally, that is to say you should exercise many different dimensions of yourself.

This gives you a brief taste of how you can work with development and meditation from a Dynamic Skill Theory perspective. Let's look at another way we can catalyze development through meditation by delving into some of the intersections of the identity development we've been exploring. We will explore these developmental structures and how they can be integrated into a catalytic meditation practice. And, as you will see, these can also provide useful pathways for developing more complex forms of listening.

Developmental Catalysts for Evolving Identities

Before we dive into identity development and meditation instructions, allow me to lay out some distinctions as to where we are going and where we aren't. As eluded to above, there are many different forms of meditation. A broad range of diverse techniques can be found in Eastern and Western orientations, religious and secular dispositions, or spiritual and psychological intentions. These diverse sets of injunctions, to be clear, are all in-and-of-themselves preparatory foundations regardless of their orienting biases.

The fundamental realization of meditation is not to do any particular meditative activity. The central purpose can be found in being the essential nature and activity—including non-activity—of meditation. This liberating realization of you as the heart of meditation is itself its own developmental vector distinct from what we are exploring here.

While a diverse body of instruction, teachings, and traditions orient meditation practitioners towards these liberating movements, we are deploying meditation to foster the hierarchical complexity of your listening skills for more effectively navigating the many social-cultural worlds you operate in. As such, from the perspective of meditative development, we can think of our training here as operating in your preparatory meditative movements. And, from an identity development perspective, we are advancing new forms of meditative training that are more explicitly developmentally tailored.

These nuances are often not understood by most teachings on meditation. Many meditation instructors and teachers are not developmentally trained. Opportunities to infuse meditation instruction with developmental catalysts are often missed. These gaps in understanding and the resultant meditative instructions can cause significant problems for some people. Others may navigate these gaps with relative ease. Regardless, joining rigorous developmental acumen into meditative training is a significant opportunity worthy of our collective exploration. This work may very well help us cultivate more robust, resilient, and mature human beings.

We are now set to explore a rare blend of meditative instruction and developmentally catalytic work. In particular, our creative synthesis may better foster identity development through the practice of meditation. This, of course, joins us back to what we explored in Chapter Two. Growing your identity development expands what and how you can listen to others.

To begin, one of the basic differentiations meditation can help foster is the separation of awareness from the activities of the mind, body, and heart. For many of us, and in many of the contexts in which we operate, the movements of the mind dictate what happens with our attention, intention, and subsequent action. In short, what you think, how you make sense of your situation, the ways you construct meaning, and how you color your thoughts with feeling drives you in powerful and pervasive ways. When thinking, attention, and intention are fused with awareness, you are largely, if not entirely, made up by the movements of your body, heart, and mind.

One of the powerful tools meditation commonly employs is suspending activity, and in some meditative realizations, most activities. When you meditate in these fashions, no matter what arises within your mental and emotional experience, you simply keep meditating. Unwaveringly you continue to employ and execute the meditation technique(s). By doing so, you begin to discover intentionality and awareness that is not tied up in the contents of your mental and emotional movements. You begin to experience a subtle yet powerful freedom from your physical, mental, and emotional activities in any given moment.

We can think of this as a form of freedom from the more habituated activities of your mind and body. If your meditation is more receptive in its basic disposition, then you may mindfully watch these movements of your mind without becoming subsumed by mental activities. Alternatively, if your meditation technique is more concentrative in orientation as in the case of focusing attention on the space between breaths, you may interrupt or suspend the usual activities you typically act on and identify with. In either case, when practiced regularly, meditation often results in differentiating awareness from most of your physical, mental, and emotional activities. At later stages of meditative development, we find not just a broader, more free awareness but an unconditioned awareness that is radically liberated from all contents.

These liberating movements unhooking intention and awareness from physical, mental, and emotional action are incredibly powerful forms of meditative development. However, as noted earlier, this is an altogether different vector of development than identity development. For example, if I am meditating from the Socialized Mind stage of adult development, then I am made up by my interpersonal relationships and mutualities. Differentiating my awareness and attention from the mental and emotional phenomena commonly found in the Socialized Mind often results in greater experiences of equanimity and spaciousness.

These greater freedoms will likely not be attributed to nor experienced as a unique facet of my distinct experience. What's more likely is that this newfound freedom will be attributed to the meditation teacher who has instructed me. Or, these experiences of a more liberated awareness could be attributed to a tradition and stream of teachings that have now granted me access to my newfound freedom. Authority, as determined by the many decades of research into the Socialized Mind, remains located outside of me in the trusted people and/or socio-cultural systems created by others. And, it is the meditative injunctions I have employed vis-a-vis others that have created my experiences of liberation.

These forms of freedom are commonly felt in response to the newfound felt distances my meditation practice instills in me. These distances are constructed from the space between my meditative awareness and the typical objects that usually drive much if not all of my experience. For example, by suspending my usual internal dialogue through a concentrative technique I feel more freedom after my meditation has concluded. I've enjoyed a break from my usual self-referential discourse and I'm relieved to have had space from the typical ways I am always trying to advance personal and professional efforts.

Similarly, if I've been meditating with techniques to cultivate greater openness then I may establish and stabilize a witnessing relationship to the types of experiences that often drive my attention, choices and behavior. Instead of acting on my ongoing attempts to take care of my important needs, tending to the people that matter most to me and demonstrating a timely responsiveness to the people around me I can just sit and meditate. I can simply watch all of these motivations, drives, and desires without lifting a finger. Again, I'm experiencing space from the typical ways of thinking, feeling and acting that often govern my life.

In both cases my meditation practice helps me to enjoy freedom from my usual ways of operating. Instead of managing and operating on my needs, or the interests of the people around me, I am liberated from needing to take any action at all. I'm freed from handling these familiar facets of self and relationship that command so much attention and energy when I am not meditating.

The all important distinction we must clarify is hiding right here in these examples. To see this key distinction, we need to recall the distinction between subject and object in Kegan's Constructive Developmental Theory that we covered in Chapter Two. You are "subject" to the elements of your knowing and organizing of experience that you are identified with, tied to, embedded in or otherwise possessed by. In contrast "objects" are elements of experience that you can reflect on, look at, handle, manage, take control of, be responsible for or otherwise operate on.

With this in mind, here are some key questions for us to explore. First, am I liberating myself from the "objects" of experience that I am already typically managing? Said another way, am I getting distance from the parts of my experience that I can usually see, am already responsible for and regularly operating on? Or, am I beginning to differentiate myself from the "subject" that typically governs my identity throughout much of my life? Am I gaining new vantage points on facets of my experience that were "subject" but are now "object?" If I am to successfully leverage meditative practices to also explicitly support identity development, then I am wise to pay close attention to the emergence of "qualitatively more complex objects."

To give you an example, let's consider my meditation practice freeing me up from taking action on my own needs, interests and desires. I may be progressing well in my meditative development as I witness or suspend my involvement in these parts of my experience. I may even begin to enjoy an unconditioned liberation from my typical everyday activities as I meditate. No matter what arrises in my body, mind and heart, I quietly abide in an equanimity not born from any outward action. However, if my liberation only frees me up from my more typical objects of experience, then the Socialized Mind would remain firmly in place.

While I may be able to see my own needs, interests and desires with greater clarity and suspend my habitual movements to manage them, I am still unable to see, as object, that which organizes me at the Socialized Mind stage of development. I am not seeing how my loyalties to the people close to me make up how I organize myself. Nor am able to see how mutualities compose my sense of self. The power close interpersonal relationships has over me is not an object in my meditation, at least not yet.

When my meditations yield the ways I am made up by interpersonal relationships and mutualities as new objects in my awareness, then my meditation practice is fostering a more complex identity alongside my meditative development. When I begin to be found by an awareness that is more free from my interpersonal loyalties, reciprocities, and co-dependencies, now I am beginning to see qualitatively more complex objects. If one of Kegan's experts in scoring the complexity of my identity development peered into my meditation, I would no longer be scored in the Socialized Mind. I would likely fall somewhere on the bridge connecting the Socialized Mind to the Self-Authoring Mind.

Not only is my identity development becoming more complex, but so would my meditative liberation. No longer am I confined to only liberating myself from activities that are enrolled in navigating needs, interests, and desires. My freedom now also enables me to suspend the forces and actions tethered to managing and maintaining interpersonal relationships, balancing reciprocities, and tending to loyalties to my lover, friends, colleagues, and/or family. This freedom would thus be qualitatively larger.

Now, many forms of meditation can likely help the emergence of qualitatively more complex objects of attention that can help foster identity development as we've been exploring. One decade-long study on the effects of meditation found a nearly forty percent increase in higher stages of ego development (a similar although distinct measure of the complexity of identity) when contrasted to three non-meditating controls groups matched for gender and age. Meditation practices can profoundly support identity development, even when instructions are not explicitly calibrated to support specific developmental maturations in identity development. However, the question remains, what benefits can be yielded by tailoring instructions to be more supportive of identity development?

These are the edges of our understanding that we venture into together in the meditation supplied at the end of this chapter. Our training is less a certainty and more an exploration into how you can support your ongoing processes of identity development through meditation. By doing so we may be able to develop meditative forms of liberation alongside more effectively growing the complexity of your identity. And we are pursuing both vectors of development to further potentiate and mature your listening skills.

Selflessness

Before we turn our attention to the practice of meditation, it can be useful to explore the value of becoming more selfless, and how distorted drives for selflessness can be significant hindrances and in some cases harmful to the ongoing development of key skills.

Often the lines between advanced stages of adult development and meditative development are blurred. This is part of a robust inquiry reaching back many decades in the West as the field of psychology has peered into meditative and contemplative traditions around the world. For example, *how are we to make sense of selflessness championed by Eastern yogic and meditative traditions? Is selflessness a regression into our infantile dispositions? Is this the bliss of a primary narcissism, as Freud proposed? Or, is the liberation from our fixations on self an actualization of the higher reaches of human nature as Abraham Maslow set forth towards the end of his life?* Today's research and inquiries are still vibrantly exploring these intersections. *What kinds of selfishness are developmentally young? What forms of self-responsibility and self-awareness demonstrate adult maturities that we ought to prize as a culture? What forms of selflessness are exemplars for our greater possibilities?* And what kinds of selflessness are impediments to our individual and collective ongoing growth and development?

Let us peer into some of the ways varying answers to these perennial questions take shape in cultures, communities, and how people engage themselves and each other. For you to better grow more complex skills, it is important for you to navigate some of the ways selflessness can hold you back. And, I want you to leverage some facets of selflessness as these experiences are critical to your more elegant listening skills.

One of the ideas that has seeped into many cultures is the notion that being selfless is better than being selfish. Look no further than parents sacrificing themselves for their children. Or, peer into many athletic coaches advocating for players to sacrifice personal achievements to support the betterment of the team. We see similar messages in many organizational cultures around the world. Spirituality and religions too, in many of their diverse flavors, often champion and popularize being selfless.

The narrative goes as follows: to sacrifice self is in some ways to advance the self's ability to participate in activities that transcend the self. Whether this transcendence is found in your children, winning or performing that depends on coordinated efforts of many people, or the realization of consciousness that is beyond form, sacrificing the self can be the price of admission.

As it pertains to meditation and the cultures that often surround meditation and contemplative practices, this narrative, direction, and intention of the benefit of selflessness often flourishes. As we have already discussed, being selfless during your meditation practice can be, and often is, essential. This is especially the case in more advanced forms of meditation.

Selflessness understood as the dis-identification of awareness from most of the activities of your body and mind can be both liberating and developmentally catalytic. However, prematurely striving to live in this state of selflessness can result in detached, or worse yet dissociative, processes that often negatively impacts both development and well-being.

For most people, the pursuit of selfless states of liberated awareness are best situated in their meditation practice. Most adults have many thousands of learning cycles informing robust abilities to sacrifice themselves to serve broader intentions beyond their self-interests. Adolescence can be thought of as a period where we learn to sacrifice personal needs, interests, and desires to serve and cohere with the emerging social circles we identify with. As such, most adults have decades of sacrificing imperial drives to serve a broader valued social circle.

As a result, many of us could be generously served by investing more in ourselves, not less. Many adults would benefit by become more self-organized, to take greater possession of themselves, and to expand that which they can take responsibility for. Self-authorship, as we have been exploring, is not only desirable for many adults, but it is functionally required to navigate many of the complexities adults face.

As a generic prescription: enact selflessness in your meditation practice, and embody self-fullness outside of your meditative training. By enacting selflessness in your meditation practice, this can mean letting go of your effort. Drop your desire to do it well or aspirations get it right. Surrender desires to get somewhere or manufacture meaningful experiences. Sit as open awareness, not a self aspiring to be more aware.

The general self-fullness I'm advocating here is not of the imperial varieties in most situations. Greater self-authorship and self-responsibility is my basic advocacy. And, let us keep in the front of our minds that cultivating selflessness in your meditation and filling out your self's robust skills for navigating the world are two distinct yet interrelated vectors of development. Being selfless in your meditation practice is a different skill sequence than the skills for self-directing pathways through interpersonal politics, economic realities, and ethical inquiries.

Selflessness off of the cushion and activated out in the world in my humble opinion is a realization or actualization of many decades of meditative development. And, it is best situated developmentally for adults who have many years of robust and resilient demonstrations of highly capacitated self-authorship or what we may generally point to as self-fullness. This enables a more complex selflessness to fully take care of you, your self, your concerns, and your issues without becoming fixated on just you. When selflessness is expressed through our greater maturities, we are able to take care of both self and other fluidly and, at least at times, simultaneously. Individuals earlier in their development oftentimes find themselves navigating dilemmas around taking care of themselves or taking care of the people around them. To do one neglects the other.

One of the interesting developmental findings we have discovered is that people much earlier in their development have "big egos." They are more self-centered, prioritize their own interests above others, exhibit greater degrees of defensiveness, and so forth. In short, people earlier in their development are more attached to themselves. Despite the frequent advocacies by the people around them, they remain fixated on themselves.

People later in their development are often considered to have "small egos." They are less self-centered, inhabit more inclusive identities, are better at taking perspectives, and are more available to serve and support others.

All of this is what many of us may expect; however, when we look at *ego-functions* we find the opposite. People with those "big egos" have small ego functions. They are more attached to themselves because they lack skills to function in a variety of ways. Thus they habitually, and often out of uncomfortable necessities, unendingly serve their more immediate self-centered drives.

In contrast, the people who we might see as having a small ego, or perhaps appear selfless, often have "huge" ego functions. They are not attached to themselves and are often massively capacitated. They are able to reliably navigate the many complex facets of life. These people are capable of making their way in the world without demanding that everyone tune to their self-centered agenda. In short, big attachments to self often mean less capable. Small attachments to self often are found in someone who is profoundly resourced and highly capable.

Many of us intuitively know this. When we really want to advance something that matters to us, we often organize around the people demonstrating the greatest skills. For those of us who miss these social signals of competence, we often organize around the people who most loudly proclaim their expertise. This is not to say that highly capacitated people can't be loud, command big spaces, captivate the attention of millions, and so forth. But, if someone can't stop being big and focusing attention on themselves, you could be served to seek someone else who can be both big and more quiet and self-sacrificing. Greater range and flexibility is often associated with greater maturities. And, as a side note, world class guidance and expertise are often accompanied by a learner's mindset, not a knower's mindset.

Now here are the two organizations around selflessness I want you to avoid:

1. Avoid being quiet and small to socially present as being selfless.
2. Avoid socially broadcasting your selflessness.

In both cases we find a self that is consumed with how it is being socially perceived. This is, of course, typical for people functioning in and around the Socialized Mind stage of adult development. However, when our socialized sensibilities become organized by a culture and community that prizes selflessness, we can run into some hindrances, and in some cases developmental problems.

If you happen to have a character structure that organizes you around being quiet, small, and not taking up much social space, consider bringing yourself more out, risk being seen more often, and present who you sincerely are. Being reserved, withdrawn, and invisible is not being selfless. Even if you're being praised for your selfless qualities, you are likely tending to a social self through your smallness and quietness. Your listening skills are paradoxically intertwined with your abilities to express yourself in diverse ways. So, consider some areas where you might be served to express more. Then, take note of what happens to your listening after you share more of yourself.

If you happen to have a character structure that is louder, where you take up more space, and you vocalize and articulate yourself robustly, take note if you're signaling the people around you to see your virtuous selflessness. Broadcasting your self-sacrifices so they can be noted in your interpersonal relationships is not being selfless. And, if you're consumed by a need to broadcast your mastery of a selfless culture—or any cultural norm for that matter—you are missing many opportunities to exercise more nuanced listening skills. Listening in more complex ways may very well lead to more skilled contributions to the people around you. And if your social standing does matter to you, elegant listening often increases your value creation and thus your more organic social standing.

In both cases there is a self that's advancing an agenda, supporting a culture, and tending to self-images and social standings. While there is nothing wrong with either strategy, if you're operating in cultures that prize selflessness, these form of selflessness can inhibit the kinds of development we're advancing together.

Bringing greater forms of selflessness outside of your meditation practice is an exquisite value. And, as noted earlier, this is an advanced developmental injunction. Many of us need a decade or more of exercising our self-directing skill sets to form the neurological foundations for more robust integrated forms of autonomy to flourish in the many facets of our lives. And, selflessness cultivated in meditation practice and activated into compassionate action in the world often takes the better part of a couple of decades of rigorous meditative training. In short, take your time as it pertains to being selfless in your life as a whole.

Now there is one caveat for us to explore. This is my sole recommendation for you to actively cultivate being selfless outside of your meditative training. Regardless of experience, expertise, development, age, profession, or context, this can be incredibly helpful:

When you are listening, be selfless.

Now, if you intend to be selfless while you're listening, you're likely to find yourself riddled with self-consciousness. Elegant listening may be more like elite athletes in the pinnacles of their performances. There's no self-consciousness. They are entirely consumed by task-consciousness. It is their immense focus and immersion into the activities of execution that drops the self. Within this flow of concentrated action, the self falls away. Exemplary listening is similar. You fall away. The more selfless you become in listening, the more full and rich your listening becomes.

So, when you are sincerely listening, for these thirty seconds, three minutes or seventy seconds, let go and receive. When the person completes what they are saying, when they pause and suspend their speech, that's when you allow the full range of yourself to manifest into the relationship. And, when they respond back, once again let yourself go. Immerse into the here and now of their expressions and articulations.

As you can see, I am not advocating that you attempt to install some selfless ideology where you aspire to be selfless in a life-long enduring way. Instead, I'm invested in your ability to become selfless, empty, and receptive for short potentiated periods of listening. Doing so will powerfully amplify your listening skills.

"AM I LIBERATING MYSELF FROM THE FAMILIAR OBJECTS IN MY ATTENTION THROUGH MY MEDITATIVE PRACTICE? OR, AM I BEGINNING TO DIFFERENTIATE MYSELF FROM THE SUBJECT THAT TYPICALLY HOLDS MY IDENTITY THROUGHOUT MUCH OF MY LIFE?"

EXERCISE 5:
THE SUBJECT-OBJECT MEDITATION

As we have discussed, if meditation is to explicitly facilitate the kind of identity development we've been exploring, then architecting meditative tools for facilitating subject-object differentiation can aid our efforts. As a review, below are the definitions of subject and object we outlined in Chapter Two. Understanding these nuances is essential for tracking and properly employing this form of meditation.

Subject	*Object*
Elements of your knowing and organizing of experience that you are.	Elements of your knowing and organizing of experience that you have.
That which you are identified with, tied to, fused with, embedded in or otherwise possessed by is what you are *subject* to.	That which you can reflect on, look at, handle, manage, take control of, be responsible for or otherwise operate on are things that are object to you.
That which is subject is absolute and immediate.	That which is object is relative and mediated.

The subject-object meditation thus has two areas of focus. The first area we call the *Subjective Seat*. Here you concentrate attention towards that which you are subject to. The second area of focus engages your attention on what we call N*ovel Objects*. Let's unpack these together and then explore some of the strategies to support your training.

Subjective Seat

To begin, focusing on your Subjective Seat means that you attend to the permeating structures of your experience that you are subject to. These are universal qualities that pervade your experience touching most or all of your experiences. For example, in your meditation you may be engaging your marriage. In each scenario that you visit, your partner's words, emotional state and other behaviors powerfully move you emotionally, so powerfully that they define you in many key ways. Your partner's actions shape your intimate experiences of who you are. Sometimes these influences are for the better, other times they are for the worse. Regardless of the context and content of the interactions, the same permeating influence persists. Here we could say some part of you is subject to this important relationship.

Instead of focusing attention into any one specific interaction, focusing on the Subjective Seat means that you open your attention to grasp universal qualities governing your experience. You're sensing into the present moment curiously attending to what's almost always—or almost always—present. You are not looking for easily seen parts, aspects or dimensions of your experiences. You are attempting to peer into the global structures that you are embedded in.

The defining features of Kegan's stages of development can be related to as helpful clues that can be used to aid in identifying the pervading structures you may be subject to. During your mediations don't be overly consumed in the theoretical aspects of Kegan's stages of development. Understanding Constructive Developmental Theory may be a helpful starting point, but abstract understandings of theory are no substitute for you growing more complex relationships with yourself and the people around you. Furthermore, Kegan's theory is likely not and the end all be all summation of that which you can be subject to. This meditation is intended to help you shift that which you are subject to—whether subsumed by Kegan's theory or not—into new objects giving you more choices and qualitatively more complex skills to enact in your life.

Subjective Seat

More universal and pervading qualities of experience that exert governance and control over you.

Novel Objects

Our second locus of focus fixes attention and engagement on *Novel Objects*. Novel Objects are structurally more complex facets of your experience from how you typically function. *These are the processes and activities that often govern and shape you.* In the above example, you could concentrate on the pervading co-dependent dynamic. In this part of the meditation you could focus on making your partner's influences on you ever more specific and nuanced. You shift this pervading dynamic into specific instances and particular dynamics in your attention. In doing so, what once had you as subject is now something you can see, manage, operate on and relate to in diverse ways.

Novel Objects require peering into harder to see objects. Just before making them object, they are quite literally the structures of consciousness doing the looking. As such, they often remain invisible. Remember, the present moment activities and processes that govern, structure, and define who you and how you function are what you are subject to. During your subject-seat meditations, your intent is to at least momentarily shift the Subjective Seat into Novel Objects. You are searching for the forces currently governing, structuring, and defining you right here and right now.

Novel Objects

Newly formed parts of experience that can be seen and felt to be exerting governance and control over you.

Objects of attention that are familiar are treated as distractions in this meditation. *Familiar Objects* are objects in your experiences that you have consistently demonstrated an ability manage and operate on. For example, spending more time in your meditation focusing on the ways you want recognition from your professional colleagues may be a Familiar Object. If you've spent years working on this dynamic in your professional development, then concentrating your meditation onto these dynamics of attention and recognition would be a distraction. Familiar Objects typically imply a familiar sense of self. To encounter Familiar Objects often invokes already established, enduring, and persistent identities. Most Familiar Objects are more of the same kinds objects that have commanded your time, attention, and engagement for years. Remember, you are searching for Novel Objects, newly forming objects that invoke novel dimensions of you.

Let's look at one important nuance as it pertains to Familiar Objects. These more routine objects can be also be new. To give an example, you may be exploring a new intimate relationship in your life. As such, this newfound love may take center stage in your meditation. Your budding relationship may be new, but the ways you are thinking, feeling, and acting may be quite familiar. So while the person, situations, and interactions may be new, these facets of your life may be related to in familiar ways. Familiar Objects—like a new romance or a spouse you've been married to for two decades—invoke a familiar you observing, struggling, managing, engaging, or otherwise operating on, or with, Familiar Objects. These kinds of objects influence, impact, and move you. However, you remain more or less the same you.

Novel Objects often feel radically different. We will focus on two classes of Novel Objects here. The first are what I call *wisps*. These are subtle and fleeting experiences that, if you weren't paying close attention, you can and often do easily overlook. Sometimes a wisp is so faint you almost don't experience anything significant or notable. Yet something novel was momentarily gracing your attention, meaning making, and engagement. For example, an inner dialogue that sounds similar to your usual inner chatter may contain a different tone and tenor. There's more authority, less questioning and a simple confidence that trusts yourself. While you may have been struggling to actualize facets of yourself like these for years, the simplicity of this inner dialogue slips into experience and out of experience almost leaving no trace. However, you noticed. You had momentarily found a voice that was able to demonstrate different qualities of insight and sureness. A Novel Object in this instance is the tone and tenor that you voice typically has. Usually there's less authority. Typically there's more questioning of yourself where confidence comes through great effort. It's the complicated nature of not being in more power that could be focused on as a Novel Object. This wisp has freed you from the confines of your more habituated ways of being and relating.

Wisps are the harder Novel Objects to grab hold of, stabilize, and operate on. They are here one flicker of a moment and may be all too quickly gone in the next moment. In my experience, these are the more frequent.

Your nuanced concentration—keenly focused on your Subjective Seat—is required to pick up wisps. When you do note a wisp, quickly attending to it is important. You are not practicing a mindfulness meditation where you let everything come and go. When a wisp graces you, attend with all of you to engage it. More on this shortly.

The second class of Novel Objects are *Sweeps*. I call these sweeps because these experiences are are often much more dramatic. These experiences "sweep you off your feet" and immerse you into different kinds of experiences. Where wisps are easily missed, sweeps hardly go ignored. The basic ground that you typically orient from shifted or is shifting. These changes in complexity are charged. They often invoke a sense of a free fall or ascension. Disorientation is common. Sometimes these experiences can be freshly liberating. Other times they are profoundly anxiety provoking. To give you an example, you may find yourself swept up into an experience at work where you feel unshakably powerful. Something in you broke, and not for the worse. The typical powers that weigh on you day-in and day-out are not weighing on you. No longer are you confined by other's expectations. Nor are you limited by the standards you typically set for your self. It's the same people, same projects and same environments but you are freer. There's a relaxation in your body and new ranges of movement that you've never experienced before. You're delighted, relieved and moving at a quicker pace than you typically do. You're seeing more, responding more organically and enjoying work in an entirely new way. Here we could say you've been swept up by something, but a key question asks, what has you now? And what Novel Objects are present? In this example, the absence of the typical power structures that almost always operate on you could be a generative Novel Object to focus on.

There are a couple of suggestions as it pertains to Novel Objects. As it pertains to the more pronounced transformative processes found in sweeps, you can easily be drawn into the emotional and somatic experiences. Attention, interpretations, and engagements typically organize around either expanse and freedom or fear and anxiety. All of these are fine experiences, but for the purposes of this meditation they are distractions.

Remember, the second locus of concentration is a Novel Object, not the secondary impacts. I say this because clarity is a state. When clarity is gone, it's gone. Stabilizing attention on a Novel Object is our chief intent.

Once you can do this, you'll have more opportunities to experience a broader range of experiences in relationship to this developmental shift. In contrast, if you get caught up in the dramatic experiences and you never stabilize attention on the Novel Object and it recedes from experience, you may have missed an opportunity for greater clarity, learning, and development.

Similarly, Novel Objects can be confused with genuinely new experiences, new insights, different ways of being, and so forth. While these are all excellent experiences to explore, we are treating these as distractions too. These could be different forms of developmentally crafted meditations. For our purposes, you are to reveal, uncover, and explore the structures that have been governing you. This meditation is not attending to where you're going next. This practice is a rigorous investigation of what has you, or more specifically, what was just governing and structuring you. You are concentrating attention on where you just came from, not where you are headed.[1]

Advancing Objectivity

This leads us to leveraging meditation to advance your objectivity. Once Novel Objects have been found, there are three interlocking injunctions. First, expand the intensity of the object. Second, stabilize the consistency of the object. Third, explore the object's novelties. I'll expound on these one at a time, then we'll get into your meditation instructions.

Intensity is related to the density and number of sense perceptions. Expanding the intensity means you are concentrating more of your sense perceptions into and onto the Novel Object(s). For example, let's imagine a wisp lightly illuminates a Novel Object in your felt-sense. Your body is telling you something key has changed. For example, in your meditation you can now feel a singular, guiding authority reigning over much if not all of your experience. To begin expanding intensity you could concentrate more whole-heartedly on this Novel Object. Feeling more acutely into your felt-sense would begin to expand the Intensity. Next, you may choose to steer attention towards your mind. What images, narratives, and/or concepts come to mind? How might you label this felt sense in your body? Perhaps this wisp emerged in a particular situation involving others; socially engage this Novel Object in conversation with or relationship to the people inside of this situation. By doing so you have shifted the Novel Object from simply a felt sense into a phenomena that's multi-faceted and even socially networked into your brain and nervous system.

I encourage you to be creative here. Engage as many of your senses as you can in diverse ways to bring greater acuity to your Novel Objects. Each time your weave in more sense-perceptions, the intensity grows and your ability to operate on your Novel Objects enhances. The more intense the Novel Object, the more potentiated you become to enact greater complexities on structures that once governed and controlled you.

Second, *stabilizing the consistency* of the object means to build continuity of experience. Instead of allowing your Novel Object to come and go, centralize your Novel Object in your attention, interpretations, and enactments. Put simply, instead of operating on your Novel Objects for ten seconds, spend ten minutes with it. If you sequentially increase the intensity as we just discussed, you'll be adding consistency as well. However, sometimes as Novel Objects are just finding their way into being part of our experience instead of the Subjective Seat of all or much of experience, we aren't able to increase the intensity. Sometimes we can, for example, only get hold of this through a felt sense. We don't know what else to do with it. All you have to do in these kinds of situations is to maintain the continuity of your experience. Consistently keep this felt-sense, or whatever sense is touching your Novel Object(s), in attention. Stabilize and concentrate on the Novel Objects. Spending more time with your Novel Object(s) advances your objectivity.

Lastly, explore the *object's novelties*. The more curious you are as you investigate your Novel Objects, the more you will learn and notice. Ask yourself, What's changing? What's happening? Where is this Novel Object going? How does it operate? What are its strengths? And, what are its blindspots? Inquiring into and keenly observing the changing nature of your Novel Objects builds the robustness of your objectivity.

When you can expand the intensity, extend the consistency, and investigate novelties, your Novel Objects will be less fleeting. And, as you more firmly anchor your abilities to operate on these freshly emergent facets of your experience, you will be rooting into a more complex Subjective Seat that advances your identity development.

Meditation Instruction

The essential structure of the Seat-Object Meditation involves three steps:

1. Invoke a Charged Experience.
2. Concentrate on the Subjective Seat (Falling In & Focusing On).
3. Advance Novel Objects (Intensity, Consistency & Novelty).

To begin, actively bring up a charged experience in your mind, heart, and body. Where other forms of meditation can treat personal dilemmas, opportunities, challenges, and aspirations as distractions, you are to surface an experience that moves you. Find a specific situation that animates you emotionally. Enter into this experience. Immerse yourself into this scenario so that you can see, feel, and otherwise sense the living contours of your scenario moving you. This can be something that's incredibly relieving, pleasurable, or enlivening. Alternatively, you may bring up a disturbing, dreadful, and anxiety-provoking experience. The important part is that you feel moved by this experience. This is Step 1 (Invoke a Charged Experience).

Remember, our intention here is to leverage meditation to advance identity development in order to evolve your listening skills. Invoking an experience that is emotionally charged activates your cognitive, intrapersonal, and interpersonal skillsets that weave together your identity moment-to-moment. Entangling your meditations into the structures governing your in-the-world identities can help foster more complex skills in the social-emotional and cognitive worlds you are operating in. While your focus in this meditation is different than in many other forms of meditation, regularly practicing the Seat-Object Meditation may also help advance other forms of meditative and contemplative development.

Once you have invoked your charged experience, bring your upright alertness and open relaxation towards the Subjective Seat that's engaged in this situation. For example, you may find yourself rehearsing an important meeting next week. Your performance matters to you and the people around you. As such, you're running through the key actions that are critical for your success. See the people in the meeting. Who's present? What are people saying? What's to be accomplished? How are the obstacles you must navigate showing up? Once you've brought this scenario to life, bring your heightened concentration into your Subjective Seat. Remember, you're feeling into the more pervading and consistent qualities that color most of your experiences. Feel into the many ways that you unknowingly repeat strategies over and over. Sense into the ways of being that you often carry into important situations. How is it that you regularly construct yourself, the people around you and the environments you are in? Curiously attending to these kinds of inquiries while you closely track your experience is an excellent way to focus your attention and engagement into your Subjective Seat. And, you are doing this from your relaxed, alert and still meditation posture.

You can expect to spend longer periods of sustained efforts in Step 2 (Concentrate on the Subjective Seat). This is not easy. I've spent entire meditation periods concentrating on the Subjective Seat without discovering any Novel Objects. Invoking a charged experience is necessary to potentiate your meditations so that Novel Objects can be more easily found. And, it's easy for your attention to become overly involved in the already visible and challenging dynamics in your scenario. Be patient and stay curious. You're looking for hidden dynamics that exert power and influence on you. For example, you might suddenly notice how your rehearsals are always tracking towards polishing yourself. You're almost always immersed in a process of expressing yourself in ways that demonstrate mastery and confidence. Maybe this was your father's project that you've adopted. Perhaps it's been your own sincere desire the past decade. This polishing process and desire for being effective could be a powerful Novel Object to work with.

Effectively executing Step 2 necessitates two key skills. First, settling into and letting go into the Subjective Seat. You must temporarily suspend your efforts for gaining visibility on your Subjective Seat. Surrender into the Subjective Seat so you can more richly experience the ways you currently organize and govern yourself. This is what I call *falling in*. It's an easeful relaxing into how you typically operate. And, how you may typically operate may not be easeful or relaxing. However, falling in involves a surrendering into the ways you naturally, without additional efforts, organize yourself and your experiences. Continuing with our example, falling in would necessitate allowing your polishing to continue. You're letting go into and allowing your desire for a polished mastery and robust confidence to fill up your rehearsals.

Second, bring your effort to see more and take notice. Foster a radical curiosity that yearns for greater visibility. Focus attention and energy onto the governing activities that make you up. This is what I call *focusing on*. Here you are probing the immediacy of what and how you are engaging life right here and now in this moment. Something that's intimately you is always and already governing, shaping and forming you. What's here? This is where you're stabilizing your attention on the various ways that you're polishing yourself and your key movements in your meeting.

The more proficient you become at quickly and fluidly transitioning between *falling in* and *focusing on*, the better quality your Step 2 will become. As your abilities for concentrating effort and attention onto precisely what you are currently doing—or were just doing—strengthen, you will be more likely to recognize Novel Objects. As you shift back and forth between falling in and focusing on, your polishing, mastery and confidence may reveal an even more embedded driver that's almost always defining you. You're terrified of failing where success matters most to you. Fear of failure governs you.

Step 3 (Advance Novel Objects) is fairly straight forward as we explored above. Focus on expanding intensity, broadening consistency, and exploring novelty. Again to advance our example, as you explore this Novel Object's novelties you may discover that you seek polished mastery to accrue validation and praise from the people around you. You do this not because you're made up by their perspectives, but because they help you mask the comparisons that are uniquely in relationship to your own standards that you are already and always failing to meet. Don't rush this (it collapses consistency). The closer you inspect your experience the more generative, diverse and unique your insights become. Again, attend to quality, not speed or quantity. You are not trying to get anywhere faster, you are simply advancing your objectivity by robustly exploring.

After you've sufficiently advanced the objectivity of a particular Novel Object, return to Step 1. You may invoke a new charged experience or you may find yourself revisiting the same charged experience although now with different areas of emphasis. You may spend your entire meditation in one cycle, or you may cycle through several times. Again, worry less about pacing. Attend to the quality and fullness of each step.

Finally, enjoy!

Advanced Meditation Practitioners

For more advanced practitioners of meditation, please note that this meditation is not intended to peer into the subjective ground of Being and Consciousness. Nor are we attempting to cultivate various forms of cessation. This is not a suspension of most activities. We aren't attempting to realize a True Self. Nor are we solely attempting to liberate awareness from the confines of form. We are not cultivating or realizing a transcending witness that is liberated from all phenomena. While you may have these kinds of experiences during this meditation—and these kinds of experiences are fine—these are not our chief purpose. These, as noted earlier, are enacting different vectors of development.

We are looking into the structures embedded in the Subjective Seat of the self that navigates the world. We are attempting to shine the light of our attention and engagement into the structures that make up how we experience ourselves and our social-emotional worlds. This meditation is "hugging" the contours of the self-in-the-world with attempts to evolve the structures of this self. We are shaping meditation techniques to potentiate specific movements that support shifting that which is subject into new objects that can foster identity development and evolve your listening skills.

6.
IDEOLOGICAL ACTIVITIES FOR GROWING AWARENESS

The formation of Novel Objects is an essential process in activating and leveraging our individual and collective potentials. The formation of new facets of experience that once commanded our choices is one of the core processes at the center of how we can change and evolve. If we are sincerely interested in the betterment of civilization, and the advancement of the relationships, institutions, and initiatives we depend on, then we are wise to attend to these kinds of innovations.

There are two places these creative advancements are likely to occur. First, Novel Objects are often unveiled in our private insights between ourselves and our emerging selves. Thus your meditation training articulated in Chapter 5 is a potent vehicle. Second, Novel Objects are often disclosed and clarified through conversation. Development is entangled with the many ways you are found in discourse with the people around you. Thus our attending to listening in general as a means to foster more robust forms of dialogue. Sincere dialogue and inquiry with those who you trust are prime locations where new ethical insights can be discovered, divergent solutions to problems can be found, and new problems previously unseen can be made visible. Your conversations can be powerful vehicles for enacting better decision-making that animates more valuable action.

The closer you look into these small exchanges—both the ones between you and who you're becoming as well as the ones between you and the people you're in conversation with—the more you will be able to participate with your ongoing development. It is here inside the small everyday facets of experience that we can imagine, develop, and enact better skills. Peer into connections with trusted colleagues, lovers, advisors, mates, clients, friends, mentors, bosses, relatives, coaches, peers, and teachers with curiosity. Look closely into the choices you are already making. Profound gateways into better possibilities surround you and are pervading within you.

We have been building throughout this book and its accompanying exercises to ready your body, mind, and heart to enact better forms of listening. You could hear more. Part of our aspiration is to gain greater visibility into the ideological constructs underlying the identities and conversations being enacted. To review, ideology—as we are using the term—is a system of ideas and ideals that are self-authored. They are creative structures providing meaning and direction in life. Ideologies are frameworks, paradigms, or worldviews that hold you together and establish a world awaiting your unique navigation. Part of our aspiration here is to be able to readily listen not to just the rich and nuanced contents inside worldviews but also to the specific paradigms and frameworks through which dialogue, identity, and choice often operate within.

And, as we explored in Chapter 2, not all adults have an internally directing ideology. Many adults have not established the Self-Authoring Mind stage of adult development as Kegan and his colleagues have studied over the past forty years. Adults who have yet to reliably self-author themselves often rely upon externally validated worldviews to be socially and culturally supplied and maintained.

Whether people are authoring their own personally tailored ideology or they are advancing their culturally supported worldviews from the people close to them, gaining visibility into the frameworks that guide us can be helpful. And, you seeing more clearly, feeling into and more intentionally relating to the processes people are are often subject to can expand your scope of listening while enhancing the kinds of responses to provide.

The intention of this chapter is to illuminate Novel Objects that can be discovered growing beyond the Self-Authoring Mind. Through investigating my own experience, curiously exploring with my clients, writing books over the past decade as well as investigating developmental literature and research, I've formulated nine interlocking features that appear to be embedded in many of our self-authored ideologies.

Explore these as possible primers. Perhaps one may serve to illuminate a Novel Object in one of your next Seat-Object Meditations. Another may enhance your objectivity on something you've already grasped but it is lacking clarity. A combination of a few of these may prove to be useful in sharpening your listening as you explore key challenges and opportunities with someone you're working with. And, hopefully these may illuminate Novel Objects belonging to your own unique emergences as you outgrow more limited ideological positions.

Lastly, for those of you who it may not be developmentally appropriate to form these as Novel Objects in your attention, read into these as opportunities and instructions on emerging facets of yourself to immerse yourself into. Keep in mind, in one reading you may be ready to operate on these qualities and in another reading you may need to further establish these skills, not outgrow them. Regardless, stay nimble in how you read these.

1. Leaning towards Difference

Leaning towards Difference is a felt sense of "leaning in" or "leaning towards" differences. Differences, divergences, and diversities in their many forms are fundamentally approached. Your physical, mental, and emotional faculties relax, open, and engage. Much of the diversities that carry charge, threat, anxiety, and uncertainty are social in nature. Differences and diversities often surface in the people you encounter. Thus a leaning towards can be felt and experienced as a leaning towards others who illuminate diversities to you. This leaning in is often gentle, soft, and patient in expressing curiosities. However, more pointed and powerful movements towards people who are different than you are also possible. Regardless of the rate of approach, your Leaning towards Difference creates and maintains forms of connection, sameness, and togetherness while engaging diversities.

Leaning towards Difference also applies to your own multiplicities, inconsistencies, polarities, and creative novelties. Leaning into yourself feels like an exploration into a multiplicity of selves. Some aspects of yourself feel more familiar, others are disowned and marginalized. Some facets of you are embedded processes while others are novel emergents. Regardless of the reason, unrecognized facets of yourself are becoming recognized and, if engaged, realized.

Just as you approach diversities in your interpersonal relationships and social landscapes, you move towards the divergences and differences within you. A plurality is often felt as a basic facet of who and what you are. And, just as approaching others fosters new dialogue and connections becoming more intimate with divergent facets, the many selves you can inhabit and express create new dialogues and relationships within you. While these connections often feel fresh, uncertain, and unmediated, you lean in towards aspects of yourself that surprise you.

This Leaning towards Difference can be juxtaposed against the felt sense of distancing from differences. Backing away, feeling threatened by or anxious about differences has been supplanted by a broader curiosity. However, it is important to note, you may very well continue to feel threatened, anxious, and uncertain. Fear will continue to visit you. In fact, with this approach, diverse emotional experiences often kept at bay are able to welcomed by a more courageous person. The touching movements of death, despair, devastation, panic, dread, and so forth are also often gently welcomed. These emotional and experiential differences too are approached with, amidst trepidation, a soft, warm, and open welcoming embrace.

2. Self-Directing Integrity

As we just explored, Leaning towards Difference illuminates an ideological positioning and identity that feels stable and durable in the face of most differences and diversities. This felt solidity and demonstrated resilience of a singular self is our second facet of experience that can be experienced. You, regardless of the challenges, contexts, and opportunities, are felt as a directing force, thus you develop Self-Directing Integrity.

Here, a persisting and consistent you is generating values. You can experience some of the ways you are constructing the measures and assessments of your life, your communities, and our world. You are forming and re-forming the values through which you filter, process, and evaluate experiences. You are authoring how you navigate the many and ongoing choices that in many ways make up your experiences and identity.

Standards and expectations are being set. Principles are formulated, refined, strategized, and executed. Your unique voice guides. Your insights, reasoning, emotions, and choices navigate the many diverse facets of your life. An inner strength can be felt. Regardless of the contexts you are operating in, there is a felt sense that you have endured, are enduring, and will endure. You possess the strength to persist. Perhaps more accurately stated, you often experience yourself to be a strength that can handle and manage. An uprightness that is felt to be you finds ways through. You are a force of continuity. Across contexts and through time, you feel as though you remain. Regardless of what space you find yourself in, no matter what possibilities you ponder or what actualities you navigate, you are a force patterning yourself, the people around you, and your world. In short, you can see, feel, and sense a Self-Directing Integrity in motion.

3. Novelty in Closeness

Another dynamic to watch for is how your Self-Directing Integrity strengthens as you approach—that is get closer to—important interpersonal relationships. Approaching the people who are significant to advancing aspirations, enhancing your fulfillment, and bolstering your well-being is an important skill to demonstrate. To approach the people that matter most to you and your values often enhances your quality of life.

With *Novelty in Closeness*, there are two types of closeness to investigate. The first is physical proximity. The closer you are physically to someone, the more influential they are in shaping your experience. There are felt differences in sitting across the table or across the room from someone and sitting right next to someone. We all know that leaving a room when someone is frustrating you brings relief. Approaching someone who you are attracted to magnifies your experiences. In short, physical proximity powerfully drives the intensity of experience.

Similarly, the closer you are with someone emotionally, the more influential they are in shaping your experience. Closing the emotional spaces between you and the people who are important to you involves being more sincere. Disclosing experiences with greater honesty and transparency creates more closeness. Unveiling and sharing aspects of yourself and your experience that you value invokes more intimacy.

As you approach and operate physically and/or emotionally more closely to the people important to you, your inner voice gets clearer. Self-guiding discernments sharpen. Insights into yourself, who you are, what you stand for, and how to navigate flourish. Closeness drives novel facets of who you are. Intimacy feels like an engine or driver for clarifying your uniqueness. The closer you get, the more pronounced your differences.

Novelty in Closeness can be contrasted against our less complex facets of identity and relationship where closeness to the people you value equates with similarities and/or sameness. Physical and/or emotional closeness can drive an unreflective agreeableness. Difference disappears. Uniqueness is veiled. Diversities are flattened into safe zones of shared biases. This is the opposite of Novelty in Closeness where closeness yields coherence, alignment, and uniformities.

4. Aspiration for Nuance

Your *Aspiration for Nuance* can be felt in your drive for clear communication. Regardless of the context, be it conflict in relationship, advancing professional opportunities, or navigating obstacles, there is a sense that choosing words with great care and intention is key for successfully moving forward. This aspiration progressively moves towards ever more specificity and accuracy in what is spoken and expressed.

In particular, problems are believed to be communication gaps. No matter what the challenge, communication is implicated. Either what was said contributed to the problem or what wasn't more clearly articulated compounded the problem. Another possibility is that what was altogether not expressed fueled the challenge. As such, you can often readily feel your Aspiration for Nuance operative in the face of interpersonal conflicts and challenges.

You can also see this drive for greater nuance operating in your attempts to draw out greater nuances in the people you're in conversation with. When someone expresses themselves to you, your first moves are often followed up questions looking to draw out nuances and enhance communication. "What do you mean when you say ...?" and "When you said this piece, did you intend to also expresses this other part?"

You can also take note of this aspiration in your own internal movements towards expressing with greater specificity. Privately, you can find yourself gaining energy by discovering more clarity. By rehearsing, replaying, and preparing for more effective interactions, your nuance sharpens. As you investigate your own expressions internally, your clarity sharpens and intentions become more transparent to you. You feel more prepared and grounded.

Implicit in your Aspirations for Nuance is a robust understanding that what you intend to communicate is not what people will necessarily receive. Intent and impact are felt as separate. Your nuance is an attempt to more skillfully join your communicative intents and the impacts you have on the people around you.

Lastly, your Aspiration for Nuance can also be felt as a drive to establish greater distinctness. Your clear and direct communication differentiates you from those around you. Your nuances highlight your uniqueness. As you peer into ever-refining distinctions, more arise. Nuance generates greater nuance. You experience yourself as a generator of nuance and specificity.

5. Remaking Experience

Remaking Experience can be a more challenging facet to see in motion; however, this powerful skill enables you to influence your experience in radical ways. When this aptitude emerges, you no longer live in a world or reality that merely happens to you. You are inherently fashioning and re-fashioning your experiences.

One of the easier ways to see this skill in action is to peer into how you reframe aspects of your experience. Reframing re-interprets your experiences in new and divergent ways. This skill uses your abilities for activating and inhabiting multiple perspectives that can enrich and diversify your experiences. Reframing opens up new pathways to advance efforts and can be particularly potent in helping groups or teams navigate change efforts, all by picking up different intentions, new perspectives, and divergent ways of making sense of current experiences.

Remaking Experience includes reframing; however, this skill supersedes operating on abilities for invoking different and possibly new interpretations. Remaking Experience also shapes perception, attention, and action. This skill makes and remakes your sense of self as well as the world and realities you enact.

Through your intentions, will, and choice, you shape attention, influence perception, and direct action to illuminate specific facets of experience.

This is likely not something you do on and off but rather it is an ongoing activity of your volition that continually influences experience. In fact, you likely cannot stop doing this. At least not yet developmentally speaking. This pervading activity of authoring, generating, and fashioning experience to better mobilize your resources is what has you. As such, regardless of what is happening, you are already in motion remaking experience to mold this moment and yourself into a more effective opportunity for advancing efforts near and dear to what matters to you.

Remaking Experience can be contrasted against the felt experience that life and experience is happening *to you*. Here you are a recipient of more or less fixed events and experiences that happened and are currently happening. And, because experience is less flexible and more fixed, less complex intentionality, will, and choices tend to focus on controlling and influencing others. A precursor for directing and authoring experience as we have been exploring is to become ever more politically astute at navigating and managing relationships as a means for shaping and directing your experience.

This controlling influence of your interpersonal relationships is quite different than you actively protecting people's more free and sincere choices. Acting on behalf of other people's sincere choices, desires, and their more genuine aspirations so that you can be of greater service to them does not impinge on what matters most to you if you are capable of Remaking Experience. Regardless of what the people around you do or don't do, you remain a generator of your unique experiences. And, no matter the circumstance, your fingers are already influencing this moment as you experience it. You're not unnecessarily pulled into managing others to influence and/or control your experience. This moment and this experience is already the opportunity to construct and fashion more of what you sincerely want and desire. Lastly, Remaking Experience often more readily mobilizes when things appear to not be moving in your favor. In the unfortunate tides life brings, you are already steering, authorizing, and influencing more of what is to come.

6. Generating Emotion

Generating Emotion is a close sibling to *Remaking Experience*. While we could treat this skill as a subcomponent to Remaking Experience, I'm teasing these apart because of the ongoing and powerful ways emotion shapes your everyday life and experience. While cognition frames emotion and emotion frames cognition, emotion remains nonetheless a more basic or foundational driver of experience. Put simply, you feel before you think. Your thinking is thus always and already colored and shaped by how you feel in any given moment.

Becoming ever more skilled at generating your feelings and emotions changes lives. And this is not just *your* life. Many lives of the people around you are also powerfully impacted by the ways you feel. Being able to intentionally generate useful emotions that enhance effectiveness and well-being is a robust gift to people, institutions, and communities. As such, let us peer into the activities of Generating Emotion.

Emotion is a vast subject. These states of body, heart, and mind powerfully immerse you into particular feeling-tones. They envelop you and construct you in powerful ways. For example, a skill you have mastered while feeling confident and in control can be disorganized or absent while feeling uncertain and under pressures you can't control. Who you are, how you think and make choices, as well as what you can do are all powerfully influenced by your ever-shifting emotions.

Here we explore but one theory on emotion. Think of this as merely one of a myriad of ways emotion operates in your life as well as in and between the many people around you. Use this as a vehicle to glimpse Generating Emotion in action within yourself. And, leverage these insights to foster ever more diverse and nuanced (Leaning towards Difference and Aspiration for Nuance) understandings of how you function in relationship when shifting emotions in changing contexts.

Emotion organizes around the implicit and explicit desires you are always and already organizing around. Embedded in your experience is an implicit assessment. Are you getting closer or farther from that which you desire? To approach what you desire generally yields positive emotions. To discover a distancing between you and what you sincerely desire generally yields negative emotions. Accompanying your appraisals are action biases. Activities of many forms are always and already in motion. And, feeling-tones pervade your experience. For all practical purposes, every facet of your existence appears to be immersed in these emotional processes.

You can see the foundational role of desire and that which you organize yourself around have in shaping your feelings and emotions. To intentionally clarify desire, authorize intent, and construct aspiration is to direct and conduct emotion. Just as experience no longer happens *to you*, emotion doesn't simply happen *to you*. Regardless of what's happening, the skill of Generating Emotion can steer that which is happening towards ever more sincere and useful desires.

While we are discussing this from an abstract perspective via language, in my experience much of this clarification, intent, and construction of identity and aspiration happens in the embodied, non-linguistic dimensions of your will's capability to illuminate new worlds through feeling and emotion. This can be felt as a re-orientation that somatically opens up different and desired feeling tones. With more self-generated feeling and emotions different worlds are formed. Interpersonal, cultural, and environmental spaces are vivified and animated for you and others to abide and operate in.

7. Narrating Evolution

Narrating Evolution means you leverage growth narratives to guide and direct your life. These are powerful stories you author and live in. They situate you and hold your desires and aspirations that revolve around qualitative changes. Some form of transformation—or the shifting of the quality or form of something—stands at the heart of *growth narratives*.

Growth narratives illuminate developmental insights into ourselves, the people around us, as well as the teams, organizations, cultures, and nations we participate in. Narrating Evolution often proposes pathways for illuminating ways your awareness and attention can become more focused, nimble, open, and expansive. Becoming ever more mindful, present, and attentive may be one flavor of Narrating Evolution. Alternatively, you may discover yourself focusing on taking more complex perspectives, networking systems of thought together, and/or integrating diverse methodologies into uniquely coherent ways of functioning. Narrating Evolution may attend to how your capabilities are growing. You contrast what you were not able to do earlier in life with the skill sets you've demonstrated to yourself and others today. And, these growth narratives shape how you desire to refine and enhance your abilities as you work on your growing edges.

Lastly, Narrating Evolution tends to not only illuminate an evolving self, but also the world and reality that is in its own evolutionary process. Socio-cultural evolution filters current events, your understanding of history, and projects futures that tell some unique version of the grand evolutionary tale of our universe.

Situating yourself amongst the billions of stars in our galaxy, or feeling our diverse cultures and the challenges facing humanity on our precious Planet Earth, can be contrasted against the parts of you that live inside of your *acquisition narratives*. Your acquisition aspirations focus on quantitative changes, not qualitative ones. These narratives track gains and losses, not your evolution. Narratives organizing around safety and security tend to orient towards preservation, conservation, defensiveness, seeking more immediate comforts, maintaining a status-quo, or following more traditional or established patterns.

In short, acquisition narratives illuminate the quantitative increase or decrease in the number of something. You are getting more money, acquiring more power, or receiving more social recognition; these are examples of the meaning-making that governs the parts of you that are not growth-oriented. Similarly, losing weight, getting in shape, shedding friends who are not advancing your current or desired social standings encase parts of you that are not growth-oriented.

Safety motivations, as they are often referred to, can be hard on you, especially if these acquisition narratives are not complemented by more sincere aspirations to qualitatively enhance who you are, how your relationships feel, and how your communities can flourish. Without skills for Narrating Evolution, your well-being will likely suffer.

8. Inward Discernment

The skill of *Inward Discernment* can be most readily visible in facing decisions that really matter to you. When life presses you up against what is most significant and important, you turn inward. When your attention folds internally, you find an inner dialogue within yourself. You are speaking to you. You hear your own voice expressing diverse facets of your dilemmas. Inside, you go back and forth, articulating the nuances you, and only you, know intimately.

Inward Discernment illuminates an innate trust in your own inner dialogue. These private conversations, deliberations, and debates try on different pathways for moving forward. As you explore your own voicing of your concerns, you listen closely to yourself. You are the best of company to the many facets of you. And, you can be your best advocate. You enact a trustable and durable confidence in yourself and with yourself. And, when the time comes to make big decisions, you are the authorizing force. You, as your own inner guiding force, direct how you make choices and move forward.

This is not to suggest that Inward Discernment does not engage others in the matters that are of the greatest significance. Quite the contrary, you are often talking to the people who demonstrate the greatest skills in respect to your dilemmas. You are often talking to many people about what's going on, how you might proceed, and the pros and cons of different choices. People are engaged, experts are consulted, and wisdom is encountered and contemplated. Connecting with skilled mentors, coaches, colleagues, bosses, teachers, friends, and the like is a given.

However, you are not fundamentally searching for the right prescription from someone else. Regardless of another's competence and experience or demonstrated wisdom and insight, you retain an inner authoritative position. You are not seeking answers from the skilled people around you. What is different is that your answer, choice, and response ultimately belongs to you. You are engaging others as a means of more skillfully finding yourself. Engaging other people's wisdom and skill helps you discover and/or create your own. As such, advice, direction, recommendations, and prescriptions of all types are filtered through your own inner dialogue and discernments. Ultimately, your path in life belongs to you. Your choices rest upon your own unique discernments.

9. Imaginative Freedom

Turning inwards vivifies your abilities for visioning, dreaming, and imagining. The more you turn inwards—that is to say the more you direct attention and energy into your own perceptions, sense-making, and choices—the more room you create inside of yourself. This increasing interiority expands your capacities for envisioning and revisioning your life.

While imagination is likely an innate intelligence embedded in the most essential movements of the human psyche, *Imaginative Freedom* activates a reshaping of your sincerities, values, and motives (and is related to the Remaking Experience discussed above). This robust capacity also demonstrates skills for remaking the socio-cultural contexts you and the people around you live and operate in. It's one thing to live and function in a pre-defined world where your imagination creates escapes from the more fixed and determined contexts that govern life. It's another capability altogether to dream and envision divergent worlds that are imbued with greater value and possibility that you and others could live into, activate, and actualize together.

Imaginative Freedom opens and broadens your interior. You feel more spacious. While specific people, opportunities, and challenges along with defined contexts are felt, the space around these parts of your experience feel expansive and unbounded. You feel as though anything is possible. You are infused with grand potentialities. Through the actualities of your life, you feel free. A bold and unapologizing freedom moves you. Inside this vast interiority, you illuminate possibilities. You as Imaginative Freedom continually discover and see novelties, creative options, and emergent potentials. You become filled with more and more choice points. Questions flourish and viable answers abound. Seemingly infinite pathways await you.

And, Imaginative Freedom often intoxicates you. You feel as though you can revision and reshape just about anything. Yet this skill ignores the persistence and insistence that is also embedded in yourself, the people, and world around you. Within this state of freedom limitations readily transfigure into possibilities. Yet, again and again, challenges persevere. Actualities endure. Continuities are unrelenting through the forces of preservation. And yet, Imaginative Freedom turns again towards the potentials and possibilities seemingly endlessly fascinated by what could be and what might become.

"THROUGH YOUR INTENTIONS, WILL, AND CHOICE, YOU SHAPE ATTENTION, INFLUENCE PERCEPTION, AND DIRECT ACTION TO ILLUMINATE SPECIFIC FACETS OF EXPERIENCE. THIS IS NOT SOMETHING YOU DO ON AND OFF BUT RATHER IT IS AN ONGOING ACTIVITY OF YOUR VOLITION THAT CONTINUALLY INFLUENCES EXPERIENCE."

EXERCISE 6:
LISTENING FOR IDEOLOGICAL ACTIONS

Listening for Ideological Actions within Yourself

Your Seat-Object Meditation practice is an ideal place to begin to mobilize your efforts to perceive with greater nuance the nine ideological activities we just explored. To begin, review one of the nine ideological activities before starting your meditation by invoking your charged experience. As you familiarize yourself with these ideological activities, you may begin by reviewing more than one activity. For example, instead of just reviewing Inward Discernment you may also review Novelty in Closeness.

The Seat-Object Meditation is practiced just as prescribed in Chapter 5. The only divergence is that you're studying ideological processes as primers that may illumine different facets of the charged scenarios that you begin your meditations with. By doing so, you'll be learning these processes more intimately by identifying their activities in the innate movements of your own psyche. Over time you'll create and compound rich learning experiences enabling you to readily feel and see your own ideological activities. As you continue learning these (and other) ideological processes, they can be related to with greater nuance and acuity.

Listening for Ideological Actions in Others

These learning foundations established in your own interior prime you to more readily listen for the ideological activities in the people you're in conversation with. Doing so enables you not only to listen for and track the content of what's been articulated, but also some of the structures of development through which they are experiencing and navigating their lives. You can better notice how they function, what skills they are demonstrating, and how these impact you beyond the explicit features of their communications.

For example, you may be able to hear the implicit activities in Remaking Experience inside a conversation with a direct report, boss, or client. Perhaps you can sense how a close friend or lover you are in conversation with is Leaning towards Differences as he navigates the challenges inherent in his own charged dilemmas. Regardless of what you notice, the basic intent is for you to progressively train so you are able to hear more. This more is not just what's explicitly stated. You are expanding your abilities to listen into what's implicitly communicated. By doing so, you'll be able to listen to, receive, and welcome more of who others are.

Listening for Ideological Potentialities

To close out your exercises empowering you to listen into ideological processes, you will be listening into ideological potentialities. For example, you may listen to a colleague unpacking how he is navigating obstacles to advance institutional objectives. In your listening, you may sense an absence of a Self-Directing Integrity woven throughout his communications. Additionally, you may also sense a gap in Emotional Generativity. These gaps or absences are not merely what's missing from what's communicated. Quite the contrary, you are listening into potentialities. You are sensing what's about to come. While someone is not demonstrating these skills, you may very well be perceiving new ways in which he could function. And, these ideological activities may more effectively solve problems, resolve dilemmas, and advance efforts. So while nothing was explicitly communicated about Self-Directing Integrity or Emotional Generativity, you may be able to sense and feel into what's possible. In some cases these negative spaces or gaps are pronounced. You might respond, "I hear what you're saying. And, what I sense—both in this conversation and others we've had—is that some part of you wants to generate a particular culture around this project, one that's your own and not mine or anyone else's. What's happening for you when I share this?"

These kinds of exchanges can be highly potentiated. You may very well be surfacing Novel Objects. And you're also inviting your conversation partners to animate novel processes and activities in their Subjective Seats. Illuminating new objects in attention and then inviting people into enacting them in their own unique ways can help foster more complex skills in the people you are in conversation with.

It is important that you are listening to and attuning for the potentialities that are ripening in the people around you. Yet you do not want to be overly invested in your own growth agendas for the people around you. Over time you will increasingly be able to see more potentials in the people and contexts around you. Many of these are for you. They are part of your own maturation process as you expand what you can sense. Only some of these are for the people you're in conversation with. In short, not all of the potentialities you're sensing into are aligned with the ripening developmental movements of the people you're in conversation with. As such, as you begin to explore listening into these spaces and responding, I encourage you to closely track the feedback. When you postulate a Novel Object, does it readily help them? Or, did you lose them? If they connect with the possibilities you're sensing into, fantastic. If not, readily drop these distinctions and come back to making contact with what matters most to the people you're in conversation with.

7.
LISTENING & SIMULTANEITY

One of the driving developmental assumptions we've been working with is that as distinct skills network together and conjoin, they form more powerful and complex skills. As we explored in Chapter 3, when you can employ both *Narrative-Based Listening* and *Feeling-Based Listening* simultaneously you can listen to and receive more from the people you are in dialogue with. Your more hierarchically complex skills can accomplish more in the same time. With some skills you can accomplish more in less time. When two or more skills join together and become a synthesis that subsumes and expresses multiple capabilities, you no longer need to sequentially use one skill followed by another. As such, a core facet of developmental complexity is *simultaneity*.

For example, in gymnastics, it is an impressive skill to complete a flip and successfully land on your feet. It's an altogether more complex skill to be able to complete this move while twisting throughout the flip so that you once again land on your feet—but this time facing in a different direction. When you can flip, twist, and successfully land with different orientations, you're demonstrating a more complex skill.

Just as our more complex and capable gymnast simultaneously executes a flip and twist at the same time, you are continuing to build distinct skills that can be enveloped into a simultaneity that will empower you to perceive more, much more, in the same or less time. Much like the foundations we already set forth, here we turn our attention towards territories or domains of experience and how you can grow increasingly complex listening abilities. Through disciplined practice, a resilient curiosity into you, the people around you, and the contexts you are operating in, you can participate with what we may consider to be more elegant listening skills.

The Deep Four & The McNamara Four

Bill Torbert is the creator of the Global Leadership Profile and the Collaborative Developmental Action Inquiry, and he is also an author of one of the most widely read *Harvard Business Review* articles titled the "Seven Transformations of Leadership." Torbert is also one of the most playful developmental powerhouses of his generation that I've been fortunate to cross paths with. One of the ways Torbert facilitates the kind of developmental simultaneity we're exploring here is through what he calls the *Four Territories of Experience*. For Torbert these are the "deep four" domains of your experience.

The first territory of experience is the perception of *the outside world*. We must "listen to" or more vividly perceive the environmental contexts we are in. We cannot get lost in or consumed by our interpersonal or intrapersonal contents. Your attention must perceive what is happening in the surrounding environments. To miss these data sets can be hugely problematic. So you must attend the environmental contexts you are operating in and that others are navigating. Accurately perceiving similarities and differences from the environmental contexts you and others live in is essential if you are to effectively understand yourself, as well as gain key insights into the people you're in dialogue with.

Second, you have *your own felt and sensed behaviors*. Each moment you are making choices and expressing these choices in multifaceted ways. This "listening" is an interoceptive sensing into your own embodiment. This rich sensory domain is loaded with information. It provides feedback to you, what you are currently enacting, and how you are showing up in your behavior. These forms of perception and experience also connect you to your own intuitions and felt-senses about what's going on around you. Your interoceptive experiences can give you useful clues and at times more direct insights into what is going on inside of the people you are in conversation with.

Torbert's third territory of experience is a mindfulness of *your own thinking processes*. This is an intentional attending to your own thoughts, narratives, meaning-making, and sense-making in general. This listening to your mental and discursive experiences tracks how you think, what you make sense of, and how you construct meaning.

Finally, Torbert's fourth territory of experience is the dynamics of *attention* itself. Here you have the ability to "listen" to the basic qualities of and movements of your attention. Imbued with attention are your intentions—both known and seen as well as unknown and unseen—which interpenetrate all other facets of you. Your attention "in-forms" what you do and how you do it, as well as powerfully shapes the qualities of how you show up.

For Torbert, the territory of experience called "attention" is neglected by most forms of adult learning. Most professional trainings and their curriculums fail us here. As a result, few us go on the profound, empowering, and necessary journey into attention itself. Torbert calls this fourth territory of experience a "super-vision" because your attention is readied to mobilize into a simultaneity, a tetra-enactment of all four territories of experience. For most adults, attending to all four territories of experience simultaneously is an overwhelming task—at least at first. Most of us simply can't do it. Our neurological architecture is limited to a more sequential approach. As you may already be seeing, just as we've been networking narrative-based and feeling-based listening skills together to form more complex and capable listening skills, you can practice employing an attending to these four territories of experience through sequential oscillations or vacillations back and forth between these territories of experience.

To support your learning and development, you can apply the oscillation or vacillation between the feeling-based and narrative-based modes of listening we explored earlier with Torbert's four territories of experience. Torbert's work is supported by sound research that points to its efficacy in facilitating more complex stages of development. So practicing with his deep four can be an important tool to help refine your listening skills and facilitate your ongoing development.

In my work, I've made subtle adaptations to Torbert's pioneering work. Here I set forth four major domains of experience that you are wise to listen to if you are to better mobilize your own potentials, as well as that of the people around you. For a lack of a better name, we will call these *The McNamara Four*.

To begin we peer into what I'll refer to as *the actual and metaphoric domain*. Your actual contexts are in many ways equivalent to what Torbert refers to as the outside world. This is an attending to and noticing of the environment that surrounds you and that you and the people around you are immersed in and navigating. However, we also join these environments with the metaphoric frames you, and others, are always perceiving through (for examples, see two paragraphs down). In short, there is not a singular fixed world out there. We are all always coactive participants in constructing many worlds that have both verifiable objective facets as well as subjective and intersubjective phenomena.

Metaphor grounds both concepts of and action in the world. These metaphoric contexts provide meaning and direction. While most people unknowingly do this, some intentionally shape how they navigate experience by more intentionally guiding their own and others' metaphoric contexts. To understand both the environment people are navigating as well as the worlds people are constructing, you must gain visibility into the metaphoric frames that are being enacted.

For example, navigating a divorce with a war and destroy metaphor is radically different than navigating a divorce from the regalities of royal nobility. The same divorce dynamics can be in play; however, two very different experiences and behaviors follow. Similarly, a rivalrous metaphoric frame guiding a board's leadership decisions is different than a board that is illuminating a cooperative non-rivalrous context to advance an institution's mission. The same company run by the same leaders navigating the same market can yield dramatically different experiences and leadership behaviors when perceived through different metaphoric contexts.

To attend to the outside world is thus simultaneously an attending to the metaphoric contexts. Not to notice the images, contexts, and implicit metaphoric dynamics is to collude entirely with already established and enacted metaphoric frames currently employed to construct meaning and direction. If you're going to receive people more fully and listen with greater elegance, some part of you must participate in their metaphoric frames and another part of you must creatively reside outside of their metaphoric reference points.

The second facet is *your own affective and cognitive domain*. We have set sufficient foundations for you to join and integrate feeling and thinking together into a single domain of experience. You are always and already embedded in both feeling and cognitive processes that are ultimately not separate.

This domain necessitates attending to your own interoceptive felt-senses, feelings, and emotion. And this domain includes mindsight into the qualities of your thinking, being, and doing. Sensing into your own images, what you're thinking about, how you are mobilizing your own energy and resources, as well as where your orienting towards are all integral facets of your affective and cognitive domain.

Third, we enter into *the interpersonal and relational domain.* Here you join together how relationships are experienced to you with what is happening within and between others around you. This is no small undertaking. We could argue that this in-and-of-itself contains some of the most complex facets of reality. Human beings can be thought of as some of most complex (not necessarily most healthy or integrated) forms of life we know of. As such, when we relate, conjoin socially, and form cultures that coordinate efforts, we have some awe-inspiring complexity unfolding in even our basic interactions.

This domain includes sensing into the embodied affective and cognitive facets of experience that are animating the people around you. Each person can be thought to be possessed by and in possession of an intrapersonal world within themselves. And these intrapersonal worlds are always and already intermeshed with interpersonal relationships that shape and in part make up their life and world. What happens here in these complex and nuanced group dynamics, cultures, and communities powerfully influences all human-directed causation, choice, and change.

Lastly, we find the *consciousness and attentional domain.* To begin, consciousness itself resists definition. However, we may conceive of consciousness here as an unqualifiable and thereby unconditioned and empty seat of awareness or subjectivity. In practical terms, consciousness can be thought of as an open unconditioned awareness that is irreducibly subjective (yet always and already influenced by objective and intersubjective contexts).

Additionally, we can characterize consciousness as demonstrating inseparable functions of both being and doing. The subjective seat of being is always and already in action. In particular, consciousness is already consciousness of something, which is at least one of its innate actions. This maintains consistency even when consciousness takes its own mysterious subjectivity as object.

Attention, in contrast, is a narrowed or concentrated form of awareness that is attending to some more specific facet of your experience. Just as consciousness implicates a consciousness of something, attention implicates an attending to something. This in some ways joins together attention and intention. To attend already implicates some intent. And any intention already influences attention.

When your attention is shaped more powerfully by your conscious and deliberative intentionality, you tend to gain greater mastery and control over what you attend to and the subsequent cascade of actions that follow. Failing to generate greater intentionality often results in failing to more effectively manage your attention. In some areas of your life, this may be less consequential. In other areas, such as how you listen and receive the people around you, the consequences are vast. Regardless, when attention and intention are not more skillfully engaged, you lose choices. Habituated tendencies flourish. Risk factors quickly compound, exposing you to outside influences, manipulations, and exploitations. When you are not more ethically shaping your own attention, intention, and the resultant lifeworld that you live and operate in, someone or something else is. In the case of ethically aligned educationally rich environments, this is not a problem. In fact this is a key part of your learning and development. In other contexts, the collapse of your choice and agency can be detrimental to you, the people around you, and the many seen and unseen contexts that are interwoven with how you conduct yourself.

Building your sensitivities to the many conscious mental states you experience helps you steer intention and attention in powerful ways. Over time, with diligence and effort, consciousness progressively opens and stabilizes. The continuity of your attention and intention strengthens. And, this growing stability of consciousness enables you to progressively steer yourself and others towards more significance in life and relationship.

The McNamara Four

1. Actual and Metaphoric Domain
2. Your Own Affective and Cognitive Domain
3. Interpersonal and Relational Domain
4. Consciousness and Attentional Domain

Typically we often bias what we do and what we say when we think of helping others, steering conversations towards that which has greater significance and value, and advancing efforts into more meaningful change. Unfortunately, these action-biases unplug you from what often may be more generative powers of how you listen and where you listen from. Quickly leaping into action, demonstrating certitude, and presenting confidence through implementing preformed decisions is a driver of significant risk in your life and for the people you work with. Privileging motion and expression costs truncated skills to receive and perceive.

Listening from each of these four domains involves a robust nexus of skills that matures your abilities for deepening receptivity and enhancing the acuity and range of perception. Each domain has the ability to powerfully shape and reshape your lived world as well as people's living experiences who are in relationship with you. As we will explore in this chapter's exercises, intentionally exercising listening from each domain provides learning cycles to deepen your competencies in each area.

And, it may be an altogether more elegant location to listen from a space of presence that is not inside any of these four domains of experience. While we can argue it's not plausible or possible to listen from outside of consciousness, it is readily possible to listen and perceive more intimately from forms of consciousness that is freed from the forms and structures of how you typically perceive. Ultimately, we are steering your listening towards a place, an always fresh location, that subsumes these four domains into a whole.

If you are not merely inside of your actual and metaphoric contexts and instead listening from a place granting you perspective on the actual and metaphoric contexts, where are you? If you are not listening from, but sincerely listening to your broad affective and cognitive contours of experiences, who are you? If you are not listening from the interpersonal spaces between you and the people around you, what are you? If you are not listening from the consciousness you're familiar with and the resultant attentional and intentional flows of your familiar experiences, where are you listening from?

Simultaneously operating on the McNamara Four, Torbert's deep four, or some other gestalt of your experiences is a life-long undertaking. Before you decided to more intentionally evolve your listening skills, you were already captured by and held in the innate agendas to perceive more acutely what is happening in and around you. And, how you perceive is already unmediated expressions of who and what you are. To listen to these domains or territories of experience altogether inside immediacy is to supplant you with the grand mysteries of who and what you are in a more radical demonstration of you and what you most sincerely value, love, and care for.

"IF YOU ARE NOT MERELY INSIDE OF YOUR ACTUAL AND METAPHORIC CONTEXTS AND INSTEAD LISTENING FROM A PLACE GRANTING YOU PERSPECTIVE ON THE ACTUAL AND METAPHORIC CONTEXTS, WHERE ARE YOU?"

EXERCISE 7:
CULTIVATING SIMULTANEITY

Development appears to follow predictive pathways regardless of what skill is being developed and where it is being enacted. After a new skill emerges—when you first demonstrate a skill—the next step marking greater complexity is to be able to reproduce this skill in new contexts. If you can only demonstrate a skill in one environment, this is less complex than being able to enact and adapt that skill to operate in different environments. For example, it's one thing to be able to demonstrate *Integrative Listening* as we explored in Chapter 3 in a professional context. It's another to be able to enact this same listening skill inside of your professional contexts *and* in your intimate relationship while you are receiving difficult feedback. Put simply, the better you're able to enact more powerful listening skills in diverse contexts, the more developed your listening skills.

Next, skills begin to get networked together. There are two steps here. First, there is a switching back and forth between two or more skills. This cycling back and forth amongst distinct skills brings them closer and closer together. The more fluid these transitions are in both the rate and ease, the more complex your skills. For example, if you find yourself getting lost in listening into the Actual and Metaphoric Domain in a conversation, you may not be able to readily track how Your Own Affective and Cognitive Domain is shaping your listening. Being stuck inside of one domain constrains both your listening as well as where the conversation can go. However, if you're able to quickly and easily slide back and forth between the Actual and Metaphoric Domain and Your Own Affective and Cognitive Domain, then you're demonstrating more complex forms of listening. This would then expand your listening as well as the range of your conversations.

The second step in networking skills together is called *compounding*. When compounding happens, two or more skills become joined into a single coherent skill. No longer do you enact one skill and then another. You demonstrate a more complex skill that operates on and expresses both capabilities. For example, when you can listen to both Your Own Affective and Cognitive Domain and the Interpersonal and Relational Domain at the same time, you've established yet again a more complex form of listening. This demonstrates a kind of simultaneity we've been working on throughout this book.

Your exercises for cultivating simultaneity are more complex than previous chapters. To begin, as set forth in this chapter, there are four distinct domains to listen into under the *McNamara Four*. We can think of listening in each domain as a separate skill to be trained. Within each of these domains, various sub-skills must be networked together if you're to be effective in any one domain. For example, you likely need both Narrative-Based Listening and Feeling-Based Listening to be compounded if you are to effectively listen to the Interpersonal and Relational Domain. Similarly, Integrative Listening is required to effectively track and listen to Your Own Affective and Cognitive Domain.

Over time, the skills enacted in these four domains—along with their respective sub-skills—are to be networked together. Transforming these separate skills enacted in each domain into one encompassing meta-skill allowing for a simultaneity that operates on all four domains is a life-long undertaking for most of us. Fortunately, you've been training your listening skills in seen and unseen ways for your entire life. And, you're likely to spend the rest of your life refining your listening skills, especially if you continue to see how powerful your listening is for advancing what's most valuable in your life.

The second challenge that is increasing the complexity of this chapter's exercises involves you creating your exercises, not me. You are going to be architecting your own exercises to train your listening skills. While I'll be setting some broader guidelines, you'll be generating and architecting your own exercises. By doing so, you'll be scaffolding your own learning sequences that can more intimately calibrate to where you are at in your learning journey. And, by authoring your own unique pathways forward, you'll be crafting ever more elegant listening skills.

Before we dive into specific guidelines to support you in generating your practices, allow me to provide one more general recommendation. Don't be overly consumed by achieving idealized aspirations and expectations for your development. Unrealistic aims derail efforts of all types. In particular, attempts to accelerate development often cost us long-term potentials. Instead of "aiming high," focus on the small. Concentrate your efforts into the micro-developmental movements that enact specific next steps that help you and the people around you right here and right now. And, developmental fluctuations are the basic processes through which more complex skills are formed. You are not linear. You are not sequential. You are a complex and dynamic cyclical organism that requires stepping forward and then back as a means of establishing trustable pathways that can be readily accessible when needed. More complex skills often require many thousands of learning cycles. This often involves gaining skills, losing them, and then re-establishing them in dynamic ways... and then losing them again. This is normal, expected, and necessary if you're to grow a more neurologically integrated brain and nervous system able to enact the more complex forms of listening we've been exploring throughout.

So, don't attempt to demonstrate these skills perfectly, proficiently, or elegantly. Attune to the subtle world of small next steps. Traffic in nuances and the little details. And, continue to steer your efforts toward the exercises that animate your aliveness and vivify your experience in the here and now. Sharpen your skills here, and foster learning by paying close attention to what's working and what's not. Effort in the ways that enrich what matters most to you and the people you're in conversation with.

Extending Skills

As you are first working with skills, one of your most elemental priorities is to extend how long you can demonstrate the skill. Can you express and demonstrate this skill into the next moment? Can you leverage this skill one more time? How can you creatively enact this skill again?

You can think of yourself as a dynamic ecosystem that is continually in the process of innovating skills. Some of these experiments into effectiveness will come and go without much or any notice. Others prove to be useful and are more likely to be integrated into your normative day-to-day functioning. As you're training your new or less familiar listening skills, simply extend them. Instead of using these skill less, try using them more.

I encourage you to use this next exercise on the fly. When you notice new abilities, different experiences, and novel ways to engage your listening, simply extend the skill or skills. You probably won't fully understand these skills from a cognitive perspective; however, you're likely to feel awkward, curious, enlivened, and/or disoriented in a helpful way. In these situations, ask people to repeat themselves or use other creative ways to give yourself another opportunity to extend the use of a freshly emergent skill. For example, you may say, "I think I'm starting to get something new in what you're saying. Would you mind saying that again?" Simple frames that invite a second pass or deeper look into something is almost always welcomed. Regardless of how you extend your skills, use this idea to help establish more accessible and reliable skills.

Diversify Contexts

As explored earlier, when you've demonstrated a skill with greater consistency in a specific environment, you are ready to diversify contexts. Expanding the range of a specific skill can involve enacting a skill in an entirely different conversation. For example, instead of using this skill with a boss or client, consider a colleague or friend who provides other opportunities to train your skill.

Additionally, consider deploying a skill into different emotionally colored contexts. It's one thing to demonstrate a skill in an emotionally neutral context. Demonstrating this same skill when emotions are big and there's charged feelings in the conversation is different. You may be in the same conversation, but to invoke a deeper sense of grief or a heightened passion in your conversations are other ways you can diversify contexts. Similarly, you may shift your own metaphoric frames. For example, instead of enacting a listening skill inside of a battle metaphor illuminating conflict, fighting and winning, try demonstrating this skill in a building metaphor.

Remember, a skill demonstrated in one area can be an opportunity to practice it again in another area. Be creative, think outside the box. Where else may this skill be useful? Look for areas where you typically wouldn't deploy these skills. How might you be able to enact this skill to generate more value? By expanding the range and enacting skills into ever more diverse areas, you will evolve your skillsets.

Switching

You have seen some of the ways I have approached the developmental movement that involves switching back and forth between complimentary yet distinct skills throughout this book and in some of the above exercises that you've been employing. Aiming for fluidity, creating balance between when and how two or more skills are enacted, and overemphasizing weaker skills are all fine strategies. What additional strategies may support you when you're ready to intentionally support your own switching between skills?

One of the mistakes we are wise to navigate is becoming overly invested in a synthesis that we can see or intuit. Remember, switching is an essential micro-developmental movement. Focusing back and forth between skills is a building block. Without sufficient switching, compounding can't happen. And, premature switching that's not aligned with your more organic growth processes can interrupt the quality of key skills that you may very well need.

Well established, reliable compounding that grows high quality skills often depends on pulling skills further apart. So there's merit in training your skills separately. Train each with rigor and your whole-hearted engagement, then switch. Immersing your focus and engagement on one skill is essential as prep for switching. Without it you risk meandering without the necessary rigor to grow more helpful skills. Once you've cultivated greater mastery in each skill, you can then bring them closer together. Play and experiment with what's helpful for you and the people you're in conversation with.

Finally, switching happens innately without effort. Oftentimes, you are switching between skills that you cannot even see. You're experimenting in ways you can't always understand. This appears to be the case for all of us. So, as you're training your skills, stay curious. You're already immersed in developmental processes that exceed any intentionality and design that anyone can create. Your curiosity will help guide you into new ways to train and grow.

Compounding

Kurt Fischer (creator of Dynamic Skill Theory) considered compounding to be the most important micro-developmental movement. It's here that we find the underpinnings of some of our best sense-making around how we become more complex and capable. To reiterate, compounding can't happen if you don't first possess the ability to reliably demonstrate two or more skills independently. Only then can they be networked together into a single more complex skill that enacts their functionalities simultaneously.

Compounding is a maturing of your skills such that your skills are becoming increasingly networked together in ever more creative and unique ways. However, this is only one side of the story. The environments you're operating in also play central roles in when and how compounding occurs. So critical are your surroundings that if the need or demand for compounding is not there, you likely won't compound skills together into more complex expressions of your capabilities.

This is part good news and part bad news. First, you conserve energy by not enacting your most complex capabilities all the time. Enacting your largest complexities all the time is not effective nor feasible. More simple tasks invoke less complex responses from you, while more challenging demands require more energy and complexity to address. This can be good news. Nobody likely needs you coordinating your most complex capabilities while you're brushing your teeth tonight.

The bad news is that without sufficient challenges that draw forth and invoke your larger complexities, you probably won't demonstrate potentials that may be important for you and the people around you.

Sometimes this is okay. Other times you may be exposing yourself and the people around you to tremendous risks.

For better and for worse, we often organize and express less complex skills until more complex responses are required. Thus we come to a pivotal developmental issue: *expectations*. We can think of expectations as intersections between you (the many diverse forms of you) and the environments you're navigating. All environments place innate pressures and demands on you. And you place innate pressures and demands on the surroundings you live, work, and love in. Expectations are mixtures of these convergences of self and world.

As you are creating, architecting, and implementing compounding practices, it's important that you establish your own sincere needs and desires for the more complex listening skills you're developing. Bring your best expectations into how you train to support compounding. Equally important is that you actively look for the ways your relationships, environments, and world need and desire your more complex capabilities. What are the expectations of the environments you're operating in? Failing in these expectations can quickly dismantle potentials. Instead of orienting in ways that can better network more complex skills together in the face of more potentiated challenges, you risk operating with more simple orientations. When you fail to respond to the more complex environmental demands, you tend to solve less valuable problems and the people around you come to know your less complex and less capable expressions of you. While compounding may still happen, it may be less likely. Additionally, compounding may happen in areas that may not serve the bigger challenges that need to be addressed.

One of the defining challenges of our time misses these key dynamics. Many of us are organized around objectives that are more simple. Yet the broader surrounding demands in our environments and world are unveiling complexities that vastly exceed current skills. All too often attention organizes around operating with the more simple problems, ones that we feel more confident in. This organizing of skills towards known problems, familiar challenges, and legacy pathways steers development into solving the wrong problems. More significant failures are averted; however, at what cost? Might we be sacrificing learning cycles that may yield compounding skills that could be vital and essential to future thriving?

As you focus on developing practices to support compounding, concentrate on recognizing the most complex demands your environments are illuminating. And, bring your most sincere and complex aspirations as an organizing orientation. Set your expectations high. And then face the most complex expectations that your environments are presenting. All of this is essential if you're going to risk failing again and again as you encounter complexities that you cannot yet operate on. Yet, with persistence and patience, many forms of synthesis await you. Creative and mysterious forces are operating in your favor, but only as you face the most significant and complex challenges you are called to be grown by.

Be Elemental, Then Build Complexity

Developing more robust listening skills within the domains I call the McNamara Four is a formidable undertaking. We can think of this as a kind of crowning jewel in your listening journey. To be able to receive deeply the actual and metaphoric contexts that illuminate the diversities of you and our world is an essential skill for understanding life. The depth and range within which you can welcome the fuller cacophonies of your human experience is perhaps a never-ending journey. However, the better you are at grasping the gestalt of your affective and cognitive experiences in the immediacy of the here and now, the more significant advantages will be provided as you navigate relationships and the diverse forms of communication that weave you together with the people around you. And, of course, listening more intimately to where attention moves and how awareness itself can yield world-shaping power for those who immerse themselves into the rigors of training attention and disciplining themselves into the rarely understood liberations of consciousness and humanity. The complexities within just one of these domains is awe-inspiring and humbling. So, be elemental. There are foundations within each domain that you already have. Start there. Then build. Sometimes you'll be working on compounding, other times extending skills. Tomorrow you may find switching useful and next week you may find diversifying contexts more appropriate. Regardless, foster your curiosities and continue.

8.
OBSTACLES IN YOUR ONGOING PRACTICE

Ongoing training, deliberate and intentional practice that repeats again and again, is a rarity in too many adults lives. Most educational offerings, regardless of the context and content, are all too commonly intoxicated by ideas. Theory, case studies, concepts, models and the like are all helpful, but alone they are often inept. Meaningful, actualized, and lasting change involves reshaping attention and consistently enacting new behaviors alongside transforming how we think and feel. It is not sufficient to do new skills for ninety minutes. Spending a week immersed in new learnings is radically insufficient. The knowledge transfer gap— the space between where you learn and where you implement new skills —is formidable. You must train. You must invoke and sustain learning cycles inside of the contexts you desire new skills. Only there in your life and relationships can new skills be more effectively grown, nurtured, and creatively deployed over time and in shifting contexts.

If you are about to finish this book, digest the ideas, and quickly move onto the next cascading ideas available to you without rigorously enacting the practices, you risk wasting precious resources. Pursuing more novelty without enacting more meaningful skills within your own lived experiences and with the people and contexts you most sincerely love and care for can be dangerous. Consumption can quickly kill your generativity. The construction of more powerful skills involves training. Disciplined and devoted training is required. Your elegance is always interwoven with how you train and with who's tutelage. Jumping from one idea to the next and leaping from expert to expert or book to book can be a risk. I'm, of course, not advocating that you stop reading, exploring, and learning from diverse contexts. However, I am pointing to a significant obstacle that cripples many people's learning processes. They don't train. Instead of pressing more fully into more effective learning cycles, too many of us skim across surfaces, skimming across one idea after another. Different approaches, quick fixes, entertaining experts, false promises, and the lure of new, different, and presumably better actions interrupt implementation that provides robust learning opportunities and meaningful traction. Novelties can quickly interrupt you, your learning, and more effective trainings.

If this could be you, take pause. Slow down. Carefully investigate what it is that you must learn to fulfill your intentions and the broader reasons for your existence. *What skills are you sincerely called to enact? What's essential for you?* Invest there. Commit and structure your days, weeks, months, and years around developing the skills that matter more and more to you. Shape the relationships and culture of your life around the people you are most inspired to grow and learn with. Unwaveringly learn again and again. Steer attention, shape and reshape your thinking, and enact divergent skills until they conjoin into the movements that are you. To fail here is to fail your hands and heart from becoming more capable of expressing what matters most to you. While there are many threats to your ongoing practice, this is one systemic issue that you are wise to successfully navigate.

Obstacles Are Opportunities

Obstacles can be hard. Oftentimes they don't feel good. What you are pursuing is being blocked in some form or fashion. As such, negative appraisals and disquieting emotions can quickly flourish. These emotional appraisals can mobilize efforts to seek safe-havens from your discord. When you distance yourself from what can be painful, uncertain, and disorienting experiences, you often unknowingly distance yourself from rich learning opportunities. Instead of nurturing efforts to make meaningful advancements, obstacles can keep you cycling in familiar behaviors that insulate you from change.

Instead of allowing obstacles to unnecessarily influence your next steps, consider embracing your obstacles. Don't distance from them. Navigate them more closely. Become more intimate with yourself and the challenges you're facing. As you approach your obstacles, remember these can be rich learning opportunities. Your setbacks, embedded limitations, and the obstinate barriers that keep you up at night can become pathways forward. More powerful skills reside on the other side of your obstacles. And the more intimate you become with what is blocking you, the more adaptive you can become. As you look more closely into the obstacles you are facing, subtle and nuanced next steps are revealed. Experimentation can flourish enabling you to better calibrate what works and what doesn't. Intimately studying what's happening and closely attending to the feedback enables you to continually advance as you more courageously face difficult experiences. And, along the way, your obstacles can shape you into a more skilled and capable human being. Obstacles can be gateways to and pathways for more powerful skills.

If obstacles are indeed opportunities to advance your efforts, then obstacles are imbued with possibilities. Obstacles can invoke your larger potentials. Regardless of where you are in your various learning journeys, obstacles can be areas where your potentials are primed. Possibilities flourish and probabilities linger in and around the limitations that frustrate and at times torture you.

All that is needed is your more sincere engagements with your obstacles. This is instead of turning away and mobilizing efforts as if another direction will get you around that which is holding you back. Consider strategically engaging with nimble experimentation. See if that which holds you back and obstructs your progress can further guide your next choices. How can you slip past? What enables you to pass through? Where can you move that advances your efforts?

Learning and development can flourish in these gaps between actual limitations and your potential actions. Your larger possibilities linger in the choices that touch both. Choice intimately born between your potential anchored through your aspirations and the obstacles that vex and perplex you are the footholds and handholds enabling you to solve bigger challenges and grow more powerful abilities. However, these rich learning pathways forward linger on remembering. You are wise to recall that this obstacle, this one right here and now, can be the rich opportunity you've been needing. Instead of distancing from the dissonance and discord, turn curiously towards the situations that trouble you. Without a doubt, potentials are right here and right there in your next choices.

Distraction

As alluded to in the opening of this chapter, distractions are significant challenges to be navigated. My good friend and colleague Scott W. Zimmerman and I are co-authoring a book on leadership and distraction right now. Distraction and a broader discussion of attention management is a huge issue we all face today. Asymmetric threats—threats that operate on you with disproportionate resources, technologies and/or information that create dramatic imbalances in power—are likely present and pervasive in your institutions, relationships, and communities. Few are adequately addressing these issues. We will save this larger discussion for our forthcoming book. However, for you and me, as we peer into the obstacles that can interrupt, impede, and disjoint your ongoing learning and the development of more elegant listening skills, we are wise to grasp hold of the basic challenges distraction brings forth.

To begin, distraction can break two different dimensions of your attention. First, distractions can sever the continuity of your attention. For example, you may be listening closely to a partner, colleague, friend, or client and suddenly you stop listening. Your mind wanders off to another conversation that's important to you. Or, your mind loops into what you want to say in response to what was shared. As the conversation unfolds, you may miss key parts of the communication. As you prepared your thoughts on how to respond or as your attention drifted to other areas of focus key, details may not have been received. Worse yet, you may receive a notification via your smart phone or computer disjointing your attention from more keenly listening and engaging the people you're in conversation with. Regardless of the origins of distraction, these unintended movements of your attention break the continuity of your listening. The continuity of attention has been split. The result is a less focused you. Concentration thins to the point that attention cannot remain consistently engaged. This cripples your ability to listen. And if you're not training yourself to listen with greater coherence and continuity, you may be unknowingly training yourself to progressively diverge and divide your attention.

The second dimension of attention distraction interrupts is significance. When you are distracted, you may no longer be attending to the more significant and enlivening aspects of your life. You may be pulled into less important and more trivial areas. When significance falters, you become entangled and engaged with facets of life that mean less to you and are misaligned from the reasons of your existence.

For example, while listening you may feel an impulse to steer the conversation in a different direction. Once taken, this direction is not one that enlivens and vivifies your experience. In fact, this different direction takes you into areas that are more familiar and less edgy. Key issues are avoided, more meaningful conversations that could explore intimate facets of the challenges you face are traded for more comfortable forms of connecting.

In this example, the more significant obstacles are not engaged more wholeheartedly. Key challenges remain unaddressed. While you may both enjoy some reprieve from more directly engaging the challenges that are troubling you both, this avoidance trades intensity for chronic tensions. Instead of dealing with the intimacies and intensities that are living right here and now between you and the people you're in dialogue with, you often unknowingly sign up for unspoken and unarticulated tensions that chronically erode your aliveness. These kinds of distraction divert the elemental resources of your attention into less impactful efforts.

To counter the forces of distraction, you're encouraged to train both dimensions of attention. To do this, you can create focus zones where you fence off thirty minutes to four hours of focus time. While you can begin with shorter time frames and progress to entire days of undistracted focus, determine what's allowed inside of these areas of concentration. Be clear with yourself about what is and what is not permitted. The longer you can sustain and maintain focus, the better the continuity of your attention. To counteract the forces of distraction, I encourage you to train daily. And be particularly attentive to when and how you interact with technology within your protected areas of focus.

Second, train your ability to abide in and operate on the most significant dimensions of your life and relationship. Paying particular attention to what enlivens and vivifies your experience is an important part of this journey. *What fuels and supports your direct experience of aliveness?* And, *what interrupts and/or numbs the amount and quality of your life force?*

Tending to the more significant dimensions of your life requires two divergent yet complimentary skills. First, you must be able to reflect. Time and space is required that enables you to get better vantage points on your typical behaviors and the ongoing patterns that often consume and govern your life. If you don't gain vantage points on how you live, operate, and navigate, you will continue to enact the same quality of meaningfulness and aliveness that you currently experience. Time and space are required to surface new possibilities. And the larger possibilities that fuel you are inseparable from new spaces and divergent uses of time.

Second, you must be able to immerse yourself more fully into your life. This is in contrast to stepping out of the ongoing flow of your life to reflect and calibrate your choices to align more fully with what matters most to you. Immersing yourself more fully is demonstrating a more wholehearted engagement with the immediacy of your life. This is a more sincere and robust enactment of the choices you've made and are making. This is the opposite of what we often call "going through the motions." This is a courageous embracing of the movements you are already committed to and enacting. We can think of this as more courageously embracing the life that's living you right now.

Together these two skills can insulate your efforts to grow more elegant listening skills. By developing a more focused self, you grow a more capable self. Leveraging your ability to reflect so that you can more courageously and skillfully embody and enact the immediacy of your life counteracts distractions of all types. With more powerful, robust, and diverse skills in the ecosystem of you, you can better advance what matters most to you.

Transmuting Agendas

Life and reality likely have broader and more powerful agendas than you do. Here, we are talking about how reality's contexts and contents has already enveloped and co-formed you. How you presently express in this moment is already a complex web of given actualities. Prior choices are already realizing and cascading as inheritances that form the world and self you presently find yourself in.

And, creativity is real. Choice is also already evident. Your choices, the ones that linger in and as the here and now have influence. Impact and consequence are also already and always in the making. While your choices commingle with the vast powers of potentiality, the sheer magnitude of the cascading interactions that subsumes and co-forms your choices likely reckons rich forms of humility.

Yet many of us are enamored by the power within our choices. You likely overestimate your influence in key ways, especially when you exert and demonstrate greater efforts with more sincerity and intentionality. And, you likely under-influence the consequences of the small choices that are expressed in all the areas you aren't intentionally focusing on. Because we tend to be biased towards our conscious intentional efforts, we often get caught inside of our own agendas.

Your agendas express what it is you're committed to doing. They articulate plans that project your choices into timelines, narratives, and sequences of actions. Agendas always invoke intended outcomes. While we tend to speak about agendas as if we are the ones who possesses and manages the agendas, we're wise to investigate whether it is the agendas that may more intimately have us. Certainly you do possess and operate on your agendas in key ways. However, they too, perhaps in more powerful ways, possess you and operate on you.

Accordingly, the ways that your agendas organize you and mobilize your efforts can quickly impede your efforts to develop more elegant listening skills. Listening in some important ways involves you dropping you. There is a radical selflessness inside some of your most concentrated and focused listening skills. And yet, there is no simple exiting from the ongoing activities that you are always embedded in. The form, structure, and substance of you is always organizing towards something. Sometimes what you're focusing on and moving towards helps you and the people you're in conversation with come closer together in more robust ways. Other times, your agendas sever the threads of connection. No longer can you know the people around you with greater nuances. You're intoxicated by your own directions.

These fixations on self are in some fundamental ways tethered to the fabric of how you perceive, and where you perceive from. And yet, as we explored in Chapter 7, you can train yourself to perceive in more complex ways that locate you outside of the conventional ways you tend to organize yourself around yourself. This iterative process of expanding how and from where you perceive will help you liberate perception from more self-centered positions. However, I'd like to offer another divergent approach that can help you work with the seemingly timeless listening obstacle our personal agendas often create.

Complimenting your skills for listen into multiple domains of experience, you can grow your ability to deepen your desires. Creating and invoking more depth in your desires mobilizes greater depths in the agendas you mobilize with the people around you. Your more superficial desires may or may not align with the people around you. Differences and divergences in our many directions often happen in the surface drives that create so much stress, discord, and conflict. However, human beings tend to have greater potentialities for coherence and alignment in our deeper more sincere desires.

If the core drives at the heart of our human experiences increasingly become more aligned, coherent, and unitive, then you will be served by deepening your desires. By infusing yourself with greater significance and meaning by enacting more sincere desires, you will progressively steer your agendas so that your listening creates ever more rich and meaningful connections. The agendas that you have and that have you carry you into all of your conversations. To listen better, to receive people in ever more elegant ways, involves deepening the desires that are animating your aliveness. We've covered much ground together, and thus in our closing movements here, it can be helpful to close with simplicities. When in doubt, when you're busy and distracted, when you're listening is failing you and the people around you, take a breath and desire with the greatest sincerities and depth that you can. Bring this whole heart more into the conversation. Listen from there. By doing so, agendas can transform from obstacles into vehicles for more robust forms of listening and connection. Your agendas can increasingly become catalysts for more meaningful exchanges.

Advocacy & Polarization

Today's world is becoming increasingly polarized. Civilization is unfortunately all too frequently fracturing into ethnocentric tribalisms. Nations are once again being pinned against each other as cooperative alliances thin under today's geopolitical stresses. Citizens' national identifications are also becoming stretched. Instead of nations organizing coherent cultures of us, many nations are internally dividing. More pronounced forms of us and them are placing citizens into ever more tenuous and delicate situations. Sadly, wherever your "us" is, the "them" presumably "over there" is getting farther and farther away. As the distances between us and them grows, so does our risks for collapsing our cooperative capacities, peace, and many valued forms of citizenship. Our capability to be coherent across differences has never been strong; however, today's world illuminates collective failures to better welcome differences. The civility many of us have enjoyed the past seventy-five years, shortcomings included, is being tested right here and right now. Around the world too many of us can all too easily report on how we're faltering. In important ways we're failing in a manner that risks animating the darker sides of our humanity. Dehumanizing each other may be just beneath the surfaces of our lives.

Dehumanization often begins as discussions and dialogues break down. When we no longer care for what others have to say, we've collapsed someone essential into something not. Unfortunately, too many of us are seeing serial monologues thrive in today's private and public exchanges. They stand in for more meaningful discourse. People express, but responses have already been prefigured. Responses are all too often not responses. They are spaces for advancing advocacies, protectors of already known and established positions. People may ask questions—even sincere questions—yet these questions often go unaddressed. Too frequently we see the monologue reign. Thinly veiled advocacies appear as if questions are being answered. With the rise of monological expressions of positions is the collapse of listening, dialogue, and lived communities that could be enacted together.

As people increasingly advocate for their polarizing positions, listening frequently collapses across these differences. The only people who can hear are the ones who already agree with the biases being advocated for. Listening is becoming more constrained. All too frequently listening operates with agreed upon dispositions. Listening is extended into familiarities. Listening commonly collapses in the face of charged differences. We only listen enough to know the "other." Then the tyrannies of polarization, tribalism, ethnocentric claims, and self-centered drives to regulate the self kick in. When this happens, suffocating allegiances, cult-like polarized narratives dominate conversation spaces.

This is all to suggest a simple point. The world around you, the cultures you operate in, and the relationships you discover yourself through may not be supportive learning contexts. You may very well find yourself training to grow better listening skills in highly challenging learning ecosystems. Systemic obstacles that effectively dismantle even basic forms of listening are thriving in many places. And yet, here you are poised to listen as a profound human elegance. This isn't necessarily going to be easy. However, you can be and become more elegant. And, these challenges alongside the many other threats to what you care for are precisely the contexts where human elegance is most likely to emerge. Ordinary simplicities, places where life is easier and the problems you already know how to solve, aren't the locations where your elegance is likely to emerge. It's in the deep and pervading challenges that have us that our larger possibilities may shift from possibilities into lived and co-discovered actualities. Whatever forms of elegance taking hold of you in the crucibles that shape your heart and what you most care for, I wish you the very best.

Thank you for taking this courageous journey together. For all the ways you've listened to me page by page, thank you. I hope these practices, our explorations here, and the learning and development you've enacted along our journey help you to advance what matters most to you. And I hope our time together here can serve the many people, institutions, and communities surrounding you.

"WHEN WE NO LONGER CARE FOR WHAT OTHERS HAVE TO SAY, WE'VE COLLAPSED SOMEONE ESSENTIAL INTO SOMETHING NOT."

ABOUT THE AUTHOR

Rob McNamara is an author, advisor, and leadership coach with an expertise in adult development and human performance. He is a co-founder of the advisory firm Delta Developmental. Rob serves on the faculty at the Ivey School of Business's LIFT Advanced Coaching Program, and he is a former Harvard University Teaching Fellow. McNamara currently advises and coaches a broad range of initiatives for individuals, organizations, and governments navigating complex civilizational-wide problems.

Rob is an Integral Zen Dharma Holder training under Diane Musho Hamilton Roshi. Rob's current areas of focus join meta-psychology, ethics, leadership development, and human performance. He's known for his big heart, radical embodied presence, and purpose-driven commitment to enacting new visions of the future of humanity.

To learn more, visit:

RobMcNamara.com & DeltaDevelopmental.com

BOOKS BY ROB MCNAMARA

The Elegant Self: A Radical Approach to Personal Evolution for Greater Influence in Life.

The Elegant Self offers a unique perspective on the future of you. Explore adulthood through a new lens as you tour the many dangers facing today's world. Gain rare clarity into some of the highest stages of mental development. Learn how the trap of completeness may be holding your influence in the world back in virtually every facet of life. Enjoy this rare invitation into the courage for you to become more of an elegant self.

- Save thousands of dollars by understanding the origin of inadequacy.

- Go beyond the limitations of the autonomous self most adults are stuck in.

- Free yourself from the trap of completeness.

- Leverage paradox to fuel greater influence and impact in the world.

- Discover never-before-seen ways to free yourself from limiting habits.

"Probing, insightful and compassionate. The Elegant Self is a life changing opportunity."

- Diane Musho Hamilton Roshi
Author of *Compassionate Conversations*

Learn more at: www.TheElegantSelf.com

Strength to Awaken: Make Strength Training Your Spiritual Practice and Find New Power and Purpose in Your Life.

This book is about the level of qualitative engagement you can bring to your strength training and ultimately the engagement you are capable of bringing to your life as a whole. Many strength training methodologies myopically focus upon the muscular system. Most fail to identify a clear methodology for managing the type and quality of attention and engagement required to optimize your greater potential. These shortcomings stunt your performance.

Strength to Awaken takes you into the new paradigm based upon training the integral nature of the human being. Readers gain a never before seen approach that restructures thinking, attention and identity in strength training to develop new possibilities. This one-of-a-kind manual connects your pursuit of Excellence with the timeless spiritual quest for awakening. Will you discover how to leverage this rare intersection of spiritual practice and strength training and access your highest levels of potential?

"One of the most important books I've seen on Integral physical training, which actually covers the entire spectrum of consciousness. It's like a combination of Rumi and a sports manual. Highly recommended!"

- Ken Wilber
Author of *The Religion of Tomorrow*

Learn more at: www.StrengthToAwaken.com

RESOURCES

Bauer, J. Park, S., Montoya, R.M., & Wayment, H. (2015). Growth Motivation Toward Two Paths of Eudaimonic Self-Development. Journal of Happiness Studies. 16(1), 185-210.

Bauer, J. & McAdams, D. (2010). Eudaimonic Growth: Narrative Growth Goals Predict Increases in Ego Development and Subjective Well-Being 3 Years Later. Developmental Psychology. 46(4), 761-772.

Fischer, K.W. (1980) A Theory of Cognitive Development: The Control and Construction of Hierarchies of Skills. In *Psychological Review*. 87(6), 477-531.

Fischer, K.W. & Bidell, T.R. (2006) Dynamic Development of Action, Thought, and Emotion. In W. Damon & R.M Lerner (Eds.), *Theoretical Models of Human Development: Handbook of Child Psychology*. (6th ed., Vol 1, pp. 313-399). New York: Wiley.

Freud, S. (1958) Formulations on the Two Principles of Mental Functioning. In J. Strachey (Ed. and Trans.), *The Standard Edition of the Complete Psychological Works of Sigmund Freud* (Vol. 12, p. 219). London: Hogarth Press. (Original work published 1911.)

Kegan, R. (1982) *The Evolving Self, Problem and Process in Human Development*. Cambridge, MA: Harvard University Press.

Kegan, R. (1994) *In Over Our Heads, The Mental Demands of Modern Life*. Boston, MA: Harvard University Press.

Lakoff, G. & Johnson, M. (1999) *Philosophy in the flesh: The embodied mind and its challenge to Western thought*. New York: Basic Books.

Landry, F. (2009) *An Immanent Metaphysics*.

Landry, F. (2007) *The Effective Choice: An Immanent Philosophy.*

McCallum, D. C., Jr. (2008). Exploring the implications of a hidden diversity in Group Relations Conference learning: A developmental perspective. (Ed.D. Doctoral dissertation), Teachers College, Columbia University, New York, NY. Retrieved from *http://proquest.umi.com/pqdweb? did=1601316511&Fmt=7&clientId=28362&RQT=309&VName=PQD.*

McNamara, R. (2013) *The Elegant Self: A Radical Approach to Personal Evolution for Greater Influence in Life.* Boulder, CO: Performance Integral.

McNamara, B. (2015) *Feed Your Vow: Poems for falling into fullness.* Boulder, CO: Performance Integral.

Moldoveanu, M. & Narayandas, D. (2019) The Future of Leadership Development. *Harvard Business Review,* March-April 2019. Retrieved from https://hbr.org/2019/03/educating-the-next-generation-of-leaders.

Scotton, B.W., Chinen, A.B. & Battista, J.R. (1996) *Textbook of Transpersonal Psychiatry and Psychology.* New York: Basic Books.

Siegel, D. (2007) *The Mindful Brain: Reflection and Attunement in the Cultivation of Well-Being.* New York: W.W. Norton & Company.

Siegel, D. (2010). *The Mindful Therapist, A clinician's guide to mindsight and neural integration.* New York: W.W. Norton & Company.

Torbert, W. (2004). Action Inquiry, The secret of timely and transforming leadership. San Francisco: Berrett-Koehler Publishers, Inc.

Torbert, W. & Rooke, D. (2005) Seven Transformations of Leadership. *Harvard Business Review.* April.

Torbert, W. & Taylor, S. (2008). Action Inquiry: Interweaving multiple qualities of attention for timely action. In Reason, P. & Bradbury, H. (Eds.), *The SAGE Handbook of Action Research.* SAGE Publishing. http://dx.doi.org/10.4135/9781848607934

Vaillant, G.E. (2008). Spiritual Evolution, A scientific defense of faith. New York: Broadway Books.

Welwood, J. (1996) Reflections and Presence: The dialectic of self-knowledge. *The Journal of Transpersonal Psychology.* 28 (2), 107-128.